W9-BNA-067

River Cutters

Teacher's Guide

MAJOR REVISION!

Grades 6–9

Skills
Observing, Recording Data, Generating Hypotheses, Using Models, Testing Alternative Theories, Controlled Experimentation, Making Inferences, Drawing Conclusions, Making Decisions, Communicating

Concepts
Erosion, Weathering, Deposition, Sequencing of Geological Events, Geological Time, River Features, Effects of Terrain and Age on River Systems, Building Up and Wearing Down Landforms, Human Effects on the Environment, Dams, Toxic Waste

Themes
Systems and Interactions, Stability, Diversity and Unity, Models and Simulations, Matter, Patterns of Change, Energy, Evolution, Structure, Scale

Mathematics Strands
Pattern, Geometry, Logic and Language, Measurement, Scale

Nature of Science and Mathematics
Scientific Community, Science and Technology, Changing Nature of Facts and Theories, Creativity and Constraints, Theory-Based and Testable, Cooperative Efforts, Objectivity and Ethics, Real-Life Applications, Interdisciplinary

Time
Eight 45-minute sessions

**Cary Sneider and Katharine Barrett
with Kevin Beals, Lincoln Bergman,
Jefferey S. Kaufmann, and
Robert C. Knott**

LHS GEMS

**Great Explorations in Math and Science (GEMS)
Lawrence Hall of Science
University of California at Berkeley**

Illustrations
Rose Craig
Lisa Klofkorn
Carol Bevilacqua
Cary Sneider

Photographs
Richard Hoyt
G. Donald Bain
Lisa Wells
Lincoln Bergman

Lawrence Hall of Science, University of California, Berkeley, CA 94720. Chairman: Glenn T. Seaborg; Director: Ian Carmichael

Initial support for the origination and publication of the GEMS series was provided by the A.W. Mellon Foundation and the Carnegie Corporation of New York. Under a grant from the National Science Foundation, GEMS Leader's Workshops have been held across the country. GEMS has also received support from: the McDonnell-Douglas Foundation and the McDonnell-Douglas Employee's Community Fund; the Hewlett Packard Company; the people at Chevron USA; Join Hands, the Health and Safety Educational Alliance; the Microscopy Society of America (MSA); the Shell Oil Company Foundation; and the Crail-Johnson Foundation. GEMS also gratefully acknowledges the contribution of word processing equipment from Apple Computer, Inc. This support does not imply responsibility for statements or views expressed in publcations of the GEMS program. For further information on GEMS leadership opportunities, or to receive a free catalog and the *GEMS Network News*, please contact GEMS at the address and phone number below. We welcome letters to the *GEMS Network News*.

©1989 by the Regents of the University of California. All rights reserved. Printed in the United States of America. Reprinted with revisions, 1992, 1995. Extensive revision, 1997. Printed on recycled paper with soy-based inks.

International Standard Book Number: 0-912511-67-2

Comments Welcome

Great Explorations in Math and Science (GEMS) is an ongoing curriculum development project. GEMS guides are revised periodically, to incorporate teacher comments and new approaches. We welcome your criticisms, suggestions, helpful hints, and any anecdotes about your experience presenting GEMS activities. Your suggestions will be reviewed each time a GEMS guide is revised. Please send your comments to: GEMS Revisions, c/o Lawrence Hall of Science, University of California, Berkeley, CA 94720-5200. The phone number is (510) 642-7771. The fax number is (510) 643-0309.

Great Explorations in Math and Science (GEMS) Program

The Lawrence Hall of Science (LHS) is a public science center on the University of California at Berkeley campus. LHS offers a full program of activities for the public, including workshops and classes, exhibits, films, lectures, and special events. LHS is also a center for teacher education and curriculum research and development.

Over the years, LHS staff have developed a multitude of activities, assembly programs, classes, and interactive exhibits. These programs have proven to be successful at the Hall and should be useful to schools, other science centers, museums, and community groups. A number of these guided-discovery activities have been published under the Great Explorations in Math and Science (GEMS) title, after an extensive refinement and adaptation process that includes classroom testing of trial versions, modifications to ensure the use of easy-to-obtain materials, with carefully written and edited step-by-step instructions and background information to allow presentation by teachers without special background in mathematics or science.

Staff

Principal Investigator: Glenn T. Seaborg
Director: Jacqueline Barber
Associate Director: Kimi Hosoume
Associate Director/
Principal Editor: Lincoln Bergman
Science Curriculum Specialist: Cary Sneider
Mathematics Curriculum Specialist: Jaine Kopp
GEMS Network Director: Carolyn Willard
GEMS Workshop Coordinator: Laura Tucker
Staff Development Specialists: Lynn Barakos, Katharine Barrett, Kevin Beals, Ellen Blinderman, Beatrice Boffen, Gigi Dornfest, John Erickson, Stan Fukunaga, Philip Gonsalves, Cathy Larripa, Linda Lipner, Debra Sutter
Financial Assistant: Alice Olivier
Distribution Coordinator: Karen Milligan

Workshop Administrator: Terry Cort
Materials Manager: Vivian Tong
Distribution Representative: Felicia Roston
Shipping Assistants: Ben Arreguy, Bryan Burd
GEMS Marketing and Promotion Director: Gerri Ginsburg
Marketing Representative: Matthew Osborn
Senior Editor: Carl Babcock
Editor: Florence Stone
Principal Publications Coordinator: Kay Fairwell
Art Director: Lisa Haderlie Baker
Senior Artist: Lisa Klofkorn
Designers: Carol Bevilacqua, Rose Craig
Staff Assistants: Kasia Bukowinski, Larry Gates, Trina Huynh, Steve Lim, Jim Orosco, Christine Tong

Contributing Authors

Jacqueline Barber
Katharine Barrett
Kevin Beals
Lincoln Bergman
Beverly Braxton
Kevin Cuff
Linda De Lucchi
Gigi Dornfest

Jean Echols
John Erickson
Philip Gonsalves
Jan M. Goodman
Alan Gould
Catherine Halversen
Kimi Hosoume
Susan Jagoda

Jaine Kopp
Linda Lipner
Larry Malone
Cary I. Sneider
Craig Strang
Debra Sutter
Jennifer Meux White
Carolyn Willard

Reviewers

We would like to thank the following educators who reviewed, tested, or coordinated the reviewing of this series of GEMS materials in manuscript form. Their critical comments and recommendations contributed significantly to these GEMS publications. Their participation does not necessarily imply endorsement of the GEMS program.

ARIZONA

Cheri Balkenbush
Shaw Butte Elementary School, Phoenix

Debbie Baratko
Shaw Butte Elementary School, Phoenix

Flo-Ann Barwick Campbell
Mountain Sky Junior High School, Phoenix

Nancy M. Bush
Desert Foothills Junior High School, Phoenix

Sandra Jean Caldwell
Lakeview Elementary School, Phoenix

George Casner
Desert Foothills Junior High School, Phoenix

Richard Clark*
Washington School District, Phoenix

Don Diller
Sunnyslope Elementary School, Phoenix

Carole Dunn
Lookout Mountain Elementary School, Phoenix

Joseph Farrier
Desert Foothills Junior High School, Phoenix

Robert E. Foster, III
Royal Palm Junior High School, Phoenix

Walter C. Hart
Desert View Elementary School, Phoenix

E.M. Heward
Desert Foothills Junior High School, Phoenix

Stephen H. Kleinz
Desert Foothills Junior High School, Phoenix

Karen Lee
Moon Mountain Elementary School, Phoenix

Nancy Oliveri
Royal Palm Junior High School, Phoenix

Susan Jean Parchert
Sunnyslope Elementary School, Phoenix

Brenda Pierce
Cholla Junior High School, Phoenix

C.R. Rogers
Mountain Sky Junior High School, Phoenix

Phyllis Shapiro
Sunset Elementary School, Glendale

David N. Smith
Maryland Elementary School, Phoenix

Leonard Smith
Cholla Junior High School, Phoenix

Sandra Stanley
Manzanita Elementary School, Phoenix

Roberta Vest
Mountain View Elementary School, Phoenix

CALIFORNIA

Richard Adams*
Montera Junior High School, Oakland

Gerald Bettman
Dan Mini Elementary School, Vallejo

Lee Cockrum*
Pennycook Elementary School, Vallejo

James A. Coley*
Dan Mini Elementary School, Vallejo

Deloris Parker Doster
Pennycook Elementary School, Vallejo

Jane Erni
Dan Mini Elementary School, Vallejo

Dawn Fairbanks
Columbus Intermediate School, Berkeley

Jose Franco
Columbus Intermediate School, Berkeley

Stanley Fukunaga
Montera Junior High School, Oakland

Ann Gilbert
Columbus Intermediate School, Berkeley

Karen E. Gordon
Columbus Intermediate School, Berkeley

Vana Lee James
Willard Junior High School, Berkeley

Dayle Kerstad*
Cave Elementary School, Vallejo

George J. Kodros
Piedmont High School, Piedmont

Jackson Lay*
Piedmont High School, Piedmont

Margaret Lacrampe
Sleepy Hollow Elementary School, Orinda

Chiyomi Masuda
Columbus Intermediate School, Berkeley

Kathy Nachbaur Mans
Pennycook Elementary School, Vallejo

Lin Morehouse*
Sleepy Hollow Elementary School, Orinda

Barbara Nagel
Montera Junior High School, Oakland

Neil Nelson
Cave Elementary School, Vallejo

Tina L. Nievelt
Cave Elementary School, Vallejo

Jeannie Osuna-MacIsaac
Columbus Intermediate School, Berkeley

Geraldine Piglowski
Cave Elementary School, Vallejo

Sandra Rhodes
Pennycook Elementary School, Vallejo

James Salak
Cave Elementary School, Vallejo

Aldean Sharp
Pennycook Elementary School, Vallejo

Bonnie Square
Cave Elementary School, Vallejo

Judy Suessmeier
Columbus Intermediate School, Berkeley

Phoebe A. Tanner
Columbus Intermediate School, Berkeley

Marc Tatar
University of California Gifted Program

Carolyn Willard*
Columbus Intermediate School

Robert L. Wood
Pennycook Elementary School, Vallejo

ILLINOIS

Sue Atac
Thayer J. Hill Junior High School, Naperville

Miriam Bieritz
Thayer J. Hill Junior High School, Naperville

Betty J. Cornell
Thayer J. Hill Junior High School, Naperville

Athena Digrindakis
Thayer J. Hill Junior High School, Naperville

Alice W. Dube
Thayer J. Hill Junior High School, Naperville

Kurt K. Engel
Waubonsie Valley High School, Aurora

Anne Hall
Thayer J. Hill Junior High School, Naperville

Linda Holdorf
Thayer J. Hill Junior High School, Naperville

Mardie Krumlauf
Thayer J. Hill Junior High School, Naperville

Lon Lademann
Thayer J. Hill Junior High School, Naperville

Mary Lou Lipscomb
Thayer J. Hill Junior High School, Naperville

Bernadine Lynch
Thayer J. Hill Junior High School, Naperville

Peggy E. McCall
Thayer J. Hill Junior High School, Naperville

Anne M. Martin
Thayer J. Hill Junior High School, Naperville

Elizabeth R. Martinez
Thayer J. Hill Junior High School, Naperville

Thomas G. Martinez
Waubonsie Valley High School, Aurora

Judith Mathison
Thayer J. Hill Junior High School, Naperville

Joan Maute
Thayer J. Hill Junior High School, Naperville

Mark Pennington
Waubonsie Valley High School, Aurora

Sher Renken*
Waubonsie Valley High School, Aurora

Judy Ronaldson
Thayer J. Hill Junior High School, Naperville

Michael Terronez
Waubonsie Valley High School, Aurora

KENTUCKY

Judy Allin
Rangeland Elementary School, Louisville

Martha Ash
Johnson Middle School, Louisville

Pamela Bayr
Johnson Middle School, Louisville

Pam Boykin
Johnson Middle School, Louisville

April Bond
Rangeland Elementary School, Louisville

Sue M. Brown
Newburg Middle School, Louisville

Jennifer L. Carson
Knight Middle School, Louisville

Lindagarde Dalton
Robert Frost Middle School, Louisville

Tom B. Davidson
Robert Frost Middle School, Louisville

Mary Anne Davis
Rangeland Elementary School, Louisville

John Dyer
Johnson Middle School, Louisville

Tracey Ferdinand
Robert Frost Middle School, Louisville

Jane L. Finan
Stuart Middle School, Louisville

Susan M. Freepartner
Knight Middle School, Louisville

Patricia C. Futch
Stuart Middle School, Louisville

Nancy L. Hack
Stuart Middle School, Louisville

Mildretta Hinkle
Johnson Middle School, Louisville

Barbara Hockenbury
Rangeland Elementary School, Louisville

Deborah M. Hornback
Museum of History and Science, Louisville

Nancy Hottman*
Newburg Middle School, Louisville

Brenda W. Logan
Newburg Middle School, Louisville

Amy S. Lowen*
Museum of History and Science, Louisville

Peggy Madry
Johnson Middle School, Louisville

Jacqueline Mayes
Knight Middle School, Louisville

Debbie Ostwalt
Stuart Middle School, Louisville

Gil Polston
Stuart Middle School, Louisville

Steve Reeves
Johnson Middle School, Louisville

Rebecca S. Rhodes
Robert Frost Middle School, Louisville

Patricia A. Sauer
Newburg Middle School, Louisville

Donna J. Stevenson
Knight Middle School, Louisville

Dr. William McLean Sudduth*
Museum of History and Science, Louisville

Carol Trussell
Rangeland Elementary School, Louisville

Janet W. Varon
Newburg Middle School, Louisville

Nancy Weber
Robert Frost Middle School, Louisville

MICHIGAN

John D. Baker
Portage North Middle School, Portage

Laura Borlik
Lake Michigan Catholic Elementary School,
Benton Harbor

Sandra A. Burnett
Centreville Junior High School, Centreville

Colleen Cole
Comstock Northeast Middle School,
Comstock

Sharon Christensen*
Delton-Kellogg Middle School, Delton

Beth Covey
The Gagie School, Kalamazoo

Ronald Collins
F.C. Reed Middle School, Bridgeman

Gary Denton
Gull Lake Middle School, Hickory Corners

Iola Dunsmore
Lake Center Elementary School, Portage

Margaret Erich
St. Monica Elementary School, Portage

Stirling Fenner
Gull Lake Middle School, Hickory Corners

Richard Fodor
F.C. Reed Middle School, Bridgeman

Daniel French
Portage North Middle School, Portage

Stanley L. Guzy
Bellevue Middle School, Bellevue

Dr. Alonzo Hannaford
The Gagie School, Kalamazoo

Barbara Hannaford
The Gagie School, Kalamazoo

Karen J. Hileski
Comstock Northeast Middle School,
Comstock

Suzanne Lahti
Lake Center Elementary School, Portage

Dr. Phillip T. Larsen*
Western Michigan University, Kalamazoo

Sandy Lellis
Bellevue Middle School, Bellevue

Betty Meyerink
F.C. Reed Middle School, Bridgeman

Rhea Fitzgerald Noble
Buchanan Middle School, Buchanan

John O'Toole
St. Monica Elementary School, Kalamazoo

Joan A. Rybarczyk
Lake Michigan Catholic Elementary School,
Benton Harbor

Robert Underly
Buchanan Middle School, Buchanan

NEW YORK

Helene Berman
Webster Magnet Elementary School,
New Rochelle

Robert Broderick
Trinity Elementary School, New Rochelle

Frank Capuzelo
Albert Leonard Junior High School,
New Rochelle

Michael Colasuonno
Isaac E. Young Junior High School,
New Rochelle

Antoinette DiGuglielmo
Webster Magnet Elementary School,
New Rochelle

Linda Dixon
Scarsdale Junior High School, Scarsdale

Frank Faraone
Albert Leonard Junior High School,
New Rochelle

Steven Frantz
Heathcote Elementary School, Scarsdale

Richard Golden*
Barnard School, New Rochelle

Seymour Golden
Albert Leonard Junior High School,
New Rochelle

Lester Hallerman
Columbus Elementary School,
New Rochelle

Vincent Iacovelli
Isaac E. Young Junior High School,
New Rochelle

Cindy Klein
Columbus Elementary School,
New Rochelle

Donna MacCrae
Webster Magnet Elementary School,
New Rochelle

Robert Nebens
George M. Davis Elementary School,
New Rochelle

Eileen Paolicelli
Ward Elementary School, New Rochelle

Dr. John V. Pozzi*
City School District of New Rochelle,
New Rochelle

John Russo
Ward Elementary School, New Rochelle

Bruce Seiden
Webster Magnet Elementary School,
New Rochelle

David Selleck
Albert Leonard Junior High School,
New Rochelle

Charles Yochim
George M. Davis Elementary School,
New Rochelle

Bruce Zeller
Isaac E. Young Junior High School,
New Rochelle

*Trial test coordinators

photo by G. Donald Bain, University of California at Berkeley

River Cutters *builds on the natural curiosity of your students. This photo, taken on a California beach, shows a familiar scene of children building a dam along a creek where it flows into the ocean. They are about to discover what will happen to the water when they complete their dam. To the children it's a playful game, but it is not unlike what professional engineers do when they plan multi-million dollar water resource projects.*

In **River Cutters**, *students create model rivers in the classroom, and compare the structures that form in their models to creeks, rivers, and lakes in their local areas. They design their own investigations and experiment with their model rivers to test theories about how water has sculpted the land over thousands of years.*

Contents

Acknowledgments

This series of river cutting activities utilizing diatomaceous earth was originated by Jefferey Kaufmann for classes at the Lawrence Hall of Science, under the title "Planet Carving." Other people who made important contributions to these activities, as first published in the GEMS series, include Jacqueline Barber, David Buller, Kevin Cuff, Alan Gould, and Cary Sneider. In addition to co-authoring this guide in its first edition, Robert C. Knott did extensive and ingenious work to simplify equipment needs and streamline activity procedures, based on comments received from educators who assisted in the testing process. These educators are listed at the front of this guide.

In 1996, Katharine Barrett and Cary Sneider, in consultation with Kimi Hosoume, Jacqueline Barber, and Lincoln Bergman, undertook a major revision of this unit. GEMS Workshop Coordinator Laura Tucker and GEMS Staff Development Specialist Stan Fukunaga (long a grandmaster river cutter), and LHS instructors Ted Robertson and Kevin Beals also assisted in this revision. Very special thanks as well to David Siegel, a teacher and geologist, for his review. This new 1997 edition is designed to more strongly emphasize key environmental issues and to update the unit in response to nationwide reform efforts, including the *National Science Education Standards* and *Benchmarks for Science Literacy*. Our collaborative work begun in 1995 with Jo Ellen Roseman and others from the Project 2061 group of the American Association for the Advancement of Science (AAAS) concerning how to determine if curricula address learning benchmarks focused in part on *River Cutters*—this ongoing process of critique has been of great assistance to us in this revision. At a later conference of the National Research Council of the National Academy of Sciences, GEMS Science Curriculum Specialist Cary Sneider described plans for this revision and gathered further input to better align these activities with the *National Science Education Standards*. In particular, we have sought to provide students with additional opportunities for reflection on how the river models relate to the natural world, and on the advantages and limitations of models. We have also recast the activities to foster learning, not only about rivers and river systems, but also to more effectively help students construct unifying concepts in Earth and environmental science, with additional emphasis on understanding the vast scale of geologic time and the impact of humans and technology on our environment and natural resources.

Also in this third edition, we include a new alternative dripper system, the "rain cloud" system, which many teachers now prefer and which is used in GEMS teacher's workshops.

Our thanks also to Susan Butsch and Eric Watterud for providing us with an excellent idea for a "Going Further" and/or assessment activity: for students to design a promotional brochure advertising the natural beauty and tourist attractions of their river area. In *Insights and Outcomes: Assessments for Great Explorations in Math and Science*, we feature a case study using the brochure activity as an assessment strategy, with analysis of actual student work and commentary about evaluation techniques. In the "Literature Connections" section, the article on using the book *Paddle-to-the-Sea* as a literary extension to this unit was written by GEMS Director Jacqueline Barber for the *GEMS Network News*, a newsletter that all GEMS enthusiasts can receive free. The article highlights one of many fine books with river-related content that can be used to enrich this unit and to artfully interweave student learning across the curriculum, meandering through literature and language arts, geography, social studies, and numerous environmental issues and concerns. The famous poem by Langston Hughes, "The Negro Speaks of Rivers" on page 20 is reprinted by permission of the publisher from *Selected Poems* by Langston Hughes, copyright 1926 by Alfred A. Knopf, Inc., and renewed 1954 by Langston Hughes. The poem on page 54 "24 Bars for a River Mural" by Robert Hass (University of California at Berkeley English Professor and 1996 Poet Laureate of the United States) is also reprinted with permission. GEMS Principal Editor Lincoln Bergman wrote the poem "Time and the River" on page 109.

The photographs of landforms in this edition were obtained from a collection of images on the World Wide Web, designed for use by teachers. Director of the project is G. Donald Bain, University of California at Berkeley. We are indebted to him and to Professor Lisa Wells, of Vanderbilt University, for permission to reproduce their photos. These and other images can be accessed at: http://www-GeoImages.berkeley.edu/GeoImages.html The image of the diatom on page 76 is by Ben Waggoner of the Department of Integrative Biology, and was obtained from the U.C. Berkeley "virtual paleontology museum," which can be accessed at: http://www.ucmp.berkeley.edu/.

photo by G. Donald Bain, University of California at Berkeley

This is Arroyo Canyon. The city of Los Angeles is barely visible in the distance. Students who live near the canyon might have spent their entire lives looking at it without thinking very much about how it was formed. A teacher living near Arroyo Canyon might ask her students to compare it with some of the structures that they will see in their first river models. The students can be asked to imagine what the hillside looked like millions of years ago when the mountains were first pushed upwards from below, and asked to imagine how rainstorms carved out the canyon, one pebble and grain of sand at a time, depositing the sediment on the plain below, where the city of Los Angeles now stands.

Introduction

Rivers, creeks, and lakes are all around us. Virtually every community can claim a flowing body of water, either today or at some time in the past. But because of the geologically short span of human existence, most people are unaware of how water has shaped their local landforms, or of the larger system of waterways of which the ones they see are only a small part.

Since students rarely have the opportunity to explore model rivers, or to get a bird's eye view of an entire stream or river system, they frequently hold misconceptions about how rivers form. For example:

- When given a map and asked to show which way the rivers flow, many students suggest that a river starts at the wide mouth of an ocean or lake and travels inland.

- Students commonly suggest that rivers flow on ridges rather than in valleys. Others suggest that rivers flow in circles.

- Many students believe that a river valley extends only to the banks of a river, and do not realize that it may extend for miles to either side of the banks, containing entire communities.

- Students have difficulty envisioning the vast spans of time over which geological changes occur, either thinking that features such as mountains and rivers have "always been there," or that they formed quickly in a single flood or earthquake.

The activities in this teacher's guide present your students with an opportunity to learn how water sculpts the Earth's surface over very long periods of time, by experimenting with models of simulated river systems. Using their models, they are able to observe thousands of years of erosion in minutes and visualize entire river systems, from the source to the delta. They observe that water travels downhill, picking up things as it goes and cutting a path to the lowest spot, where it then accumulates as a lake or ocean. They see how rivers create landforms, such as canyons, forks, meandering channels, and deltas. They also use their models to test alternative theories about how different river features are formed and how humans can and do impact river systems. By observing and recording results, students begin to understand rivers as dynamic, ever-changing systems.

Newly Aligned with Standards and Benchmarks

As described in more detail in the Acknowledgments, River Cutters has undergone a comprehensive review and revision process to better support and convey content, goals, and recommendations of the National Science Education Standards, Benchmarks for Science Literacy, *and other leading guidelines for curricular excellence in science and mathematics.*

Stories in Stone, *a GEMS guide for Grades 4–9, further explores geology and the forces that shape the earth, including activities about the processes that produce igneous, sedimentary, and metamorphic rocks, the rock cycle, and tectonic plate theory.* Stories in Stone *would make a great partner to* River Cutters. *One teacher set up a river cutting system as a demonstration during the* Stories in Stone *unit.*

photo by G. Donald Bain, University of California at Berkeley

In the River Cutters *models, two rivers running parallel sometimes join into one channel. This happens in the real world too, as shown in this photo of the confluence of the Eel River and the Middle Fork of the Eel River.*

If you and your students have access to the internet, you'll find many photographs of river features. Many of the photos in the guide can be found at: http://www-GeoImages.berkeley.edu/ GeoImages.html

In addition to learning to identify geological formations, your students will develop vocabulary related to river geology, and refine skills that they will need for continued study in science. These skills include: observing, recording data, generating hypotheses, using models, testing alternative theories, experimenting, making inferences, drawing conclusions, making decisions, and communicating.

This unit also provides a stimulating introduction to a number of important environmental issues, as your students use their models to explore the effects of human activities on river systems. They observe the effects of building a dam, and they model what occurs when a leaky toxic waste dump pollutes the watershed. Students also have opportunities to explore other environmental issues, such as increased erosion due to land use patterns, or building on flood plains.

How can *River Cutters* fit into your curriculum plan? If you are emphasizing fundamental concepts in **Earth Science**, *River Cutters* will help your students understand the forces that shape the earth, such as erosion, weathering, and deposition, as well as the sequencing of geological events. If you aim to present a course in **Environmental Studies**, *River Cutters* will provide your students with hands-on activities that illustrate how certain human activities impact natural systems. If your curriculum emphasizes **Integrated Science**, *River Cutters* can help students apply concepts in physical, Earth, and environmental sciences to real world problems, thus spreading a delta across the curriculum.

Session by Session

Although *River Cutters* can be conducted in nine class periods, it's better to arrange four or five double periods, so students can reflect immediately after they've created their rivers. If double lab periods are not possible, and when consecutive groups of students will use the materials, it's especially important for students to sketch their rivers, to refer to during the next class session.

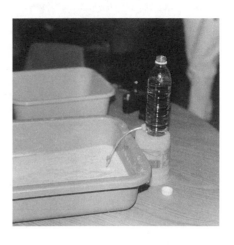

Session 1: Exploring a Model River. The first session invites students to explain how they think the local landscape was created. This both generates interest and helps you find out their initial ideas. You demonstrate how to use the materials and students cut their first model rivers. This free exploration enables your students to see the intricate "river systems" they can create in minutes and sets the stage for later more controlled studies. As students create their first rivers and sketch the results, you can assess prior knowledge and river-related vocabulary.

Session 2: Discussing River Features. Students refer to drawings of their river models and discuss how some features they observed may be seen in their own region. They compare their drawings with photos and diagrams on the "Geological Features" handout, and with pictures of landscapes. The class generates a list of river features they observed. Forces that build up and tear down the landscape are discussed.

Session 3: Time and the River. Nearly everyone needs help in comprehending how long it has taken for geological features to develop. This activity provides a variety of ways for students to visualize geologic time by relating their own lifetime to the river model and by comparing geological and historical events. The session also increases student knowledge of the geologic and climate history of our home planet.

The Green River (top) and the Sacramento River (bottom) have both cut meandering river valleys—but the Green River Valley is much deeper than the Sacramento Valley. Why?

Session 4: Dams and Toxic Waste. This investigation shows how rivers change over geologic time, *and* how human intervention can change river systems. Students conduct a five-minute river run (representing 5,000 years of erosion and deposition). They position marker flags next to features, draw the river systems, and reflect on how the rivers changed with no human intervention over "thousands" of years. They then build model dams and place simulated toxic waste dumps along the watershed, re-start the rivers, and observe changes for five more minutes (in this case representing 50 years of human intervention). They draw how the rivers now appear. This activity also emphasizes the importance of systematic observation and of recording how the model changes over time, as students gather evidence for discussion in the next session.

photos by Lisa Wells, Vanderbilt University

photo by Lisa Wells, Vanderbilt University

Undercut waterfall. A soft layer of rock at a deeper level has been undercut by the constantly flowing water. In time, the upper layer will break away, then the deeper layer will erode some more. Over thousands of years, the waterfall will migrate upstream.

Model: a representation of an object or process.

Variable: Something that can be changed.

Controlled experiment: a "fair test" that can be used to compare two theories or predictions. All variables are kept the same, except for the test variable.

Session 5: Discussing the Results of River Models.
Students discuss the results of the previous session, and consider how their ideas may apply to real rivers today. The discussion of the results naturally leads to more wide-ranging discussions concerning the environmental impacts of technology and human interference on river systems. Benefits and drawbacks of such interference are considered and strong real-life connections are made as students debate questions like those certain to arise as they become responsible citizens of the 21st century. Students may want further investigate some of these questions using their models in Session 7.

Session 6: River Experiments: Age or Slope?
This session provides further practice in observing and recording changes in model river systems. It also introduces a more sophisticated laboratory method—controlled experimentation aimed at testing alternative theories. First, the students look at pictures and photographs of the Green and the Sacramento River Valleys, and discuss their own theories for why one is so deep and the other so broad and shallow. They then conduct a controlled experiment to compare two alternative theories: that the difference between these two rivers is due to differences in the *ages* of the rivers, versus the idea that it is caused by differences in the *slope* of the terrain. Students discuss their results and learn about additional evidence to resolve the question of how these rivers were formed. At the end of the session the students reflect on how they used their models to conduct a fair test to determine which of two different theories provided a better explanation.

Session 7: Designing Your Own Experiments.
The final activity, in which students design their own investigations, is an opportunity for the students to apply what they have learned to something they care about. The students start by selecting a question they wish to explore and decide how to use their model rivers to learn something about that question. The students may draw from suggestions offered by the teacher, or they may explore issues that have arisen during their earlier investigations.

Encourage the students to think about the method that is most appropriate for their specific investigation—e.g., systematic observation and recording, a comparison, or a controlled experiment. We suggest that this last session be split into three class periods: one to plan their experiments, one to conduct the experiment using the river models, and a final period for each group of students to report on the results of their experiments.

Well Worth the Preparation

At least several thousand teachers have presented *River Cutters* since it was released in 1989. A number of science centers and water resource boards have used the guide and praised its educational value and great student appeal. Many teachers who have written to us about their positive experiences have told a similar story. "It's messy, and it takes a lot of preparation, but it's worth it!" As you decide whether or not to include *River Cutters* in your curriculum, it's important to consider these two factors— the preparation time and the mess.

Preparation Time. The initial preparation time for this series of activities is substantial, but many teachers have found the educational value well worth the effort. Literally thousands of classroom teachers, science and environmental educators nationwide have testified to the combination of excitement and solid content. In this revised edition, we have been especially attentive to pointing out the opportunities embedded in *River Cutters* to help students construct more advanced knowledge in the earth sciences, technology, and the environment, and in using a working model as a tool for investigation. We strongly encourage you to enlist aides, parents, and student assistants as classroom volunteers to help you prepare and to help the students during the laboratory periods. An extra pair of hands can make a world of difference. Depending on the capabilities of your students, you can also involve them in much of the initial preparation. This unit is a natural and rewarding way to encourage the involvement of parents or other concerned adults or community members in education. Environmental and water resource organizations or agencies in your area could also be called upon to make presentations on local issues and career pathways.

The Mess. Yes, it's messy, but there are things you can do to reduce it. The easiest way is to do the activities outdoors on picnic tables. When finished, bring the tubs indoors then hose down the tables. If you have to work indoors, you'll probably find white spots all over the room a couple of hours after the activity. When dry, these spots can be quickly wiped or vacuumed up. Water containing a small amount of diatomaceous earth may be poured down the drain, as long as it is flushed well with water. We suggest that you cover any computers or optical equipment you may have in the room during the activity.

This river flows through a mountainous region. Rain erodes the surrounding slopes, forming erosion gullies where weathered rock and soil are washed into the river below. The swiftly-flowing river quickly carries the sediment downstream, where it is eventually deposited when the river slows down—perhaps on a floodplain, lake bottom, delta, or the ocean floor. Over thousands of years, the V-shaped valley is cut deeper and deeper.

photo by Lisa Wells, Vanderbilt University

Many teachers enlist students' help. Leave ten minutes at the end of each session for your students to clean up their stations. Emphasize that the diatomaceous earth should remain in the tubs. Some teachers like to make a universal "No Mess" sign, and to tell the class that each student team is responsible for cleaning up their own work area.

As one student put it, "this activity is the messiest, but it's also the funnest." Students become very involved and excited in all phases of these river-cutting activities. Also, the activities can provide your students with a unique level of understanding about geological concepts that would not be possible to achieve with reading or computer simulations alone. So roll up your sleeves and get ready to create a river!

Time Frame

Please note: The times listed above are approximations, based on teaching experience in a variety of classroom situations. However, some teachers may need or want to spend more time on certain parts of this activity, depending on class size, grade level, student interest, curriculum emphasis, and numerous other factors.

photo by Lisa Wells, Vanderbilt University

Only a trickle of water runs through this valley today, but at other times of the year the river runs full, and sometimes floods. The valley as a whole was shaped by the river over tens of thousands of years. Much of the sandy material that now forms the valley floor was transported by fast-running streams in the distant mountains.

What You Need (for all sessions)

Non-Consumables

- ❑ 1 *River Cutters* Teacher's Guide
- ❑ 1 disposable dust mask
- ❑ 1 measuring cup, 1 qt. (1 liter) capacity
- ❑ 2 pitchers, about 2 qts. (2 liters) each
- ❑ 1 bucket
- ❑ 5–8 sturdy plastic tubs, 5"–7" (12–18 cm) deep, at least 20" (50 cm) long, and 15" (38 cm) wide. We recommend restaurant dish bussing tubs.
- ❑ 5–8 sponges, about 1" x 3" x 5" (2 cm x 8 cm x 13 cm)
- ❑ 5–8 aluminum pie pans, 9" (23 cm) diam.
- ❑ 5–8 pieces of wood, 8" lengths of two-by-four or children's large wooden blocks
- ❑ 5–8 dripper systems. See pages 13–15 and choose **either** the Rain Cloud dripper system **or** the Siphon dripper system. Collect the materials you will need for one dripper per team:

Either For **each** Rain Cloud dripper system:
- ❑ 1 plastic water bottle with cap, 1 pt. to 1 qt. size
- ❑ silicone caulk (the type that remains flexible when dry) or hot glue gun
- ❑ 1 3" –5" piece of flexible aquarium air hose
- ❑ 1 adjustable plastic aquarium control valve
- ❑ 1 Phillips screwdriver, medium to large size (slightly smaller than the diameter of the aquarium hose), one for all dripper systems
- ❑ 1 cigarette lighter, candle, or gas stove for heating screwdriver to melt a hole in plastic bottle
- ❑ 1 metal coffee can, sturdy box, or plastic container to support the plastic bottle 8"–10" (20 cm x 25 cm) above the table (the piece of wood used to slope the diatomaceous earth can also be used)

Optional:
- ❑ 1 "T" valve that fits inside the air hose, as an additional valve, to run two rivers at the same time
- ❑ 1 additional adjustable plastic aquarium control valve
- ❑ 1 spray bottle of water—to simulate rain over an entire watershed

Or For **each** Siphon dripper system:
- ❑ 1 wide-mouthed, tapered, 9 oz. soft plastic cup (270 ml) with notch cut on edge
- ❑ 1 plastic stir stick with two small holes (commonly used as coffee stirrers)
- ❑ 1 piece of wire, 4" (10 cm) long (20 gauge or .035" in diam.), small enough to go through one hole in the stir stick
- ❑ 1 small squeeze bottle of liquid detergent

© 1997 by The Regents of the University of California. LHS GEMS: *River Cutters.*   (*List continued on page 10.*)

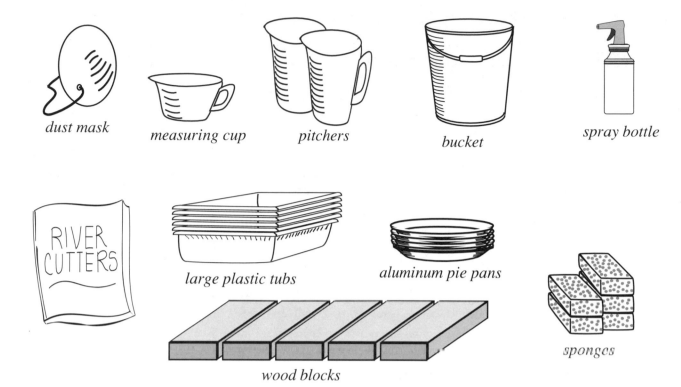

dust mask measuring cup pitchers bucket spray bottle

RIVER CUTTERS

large plastic tubs aluminum pie pans

wood blocks sponges

*Materials needed for **each** Rain Cloud dripper system*

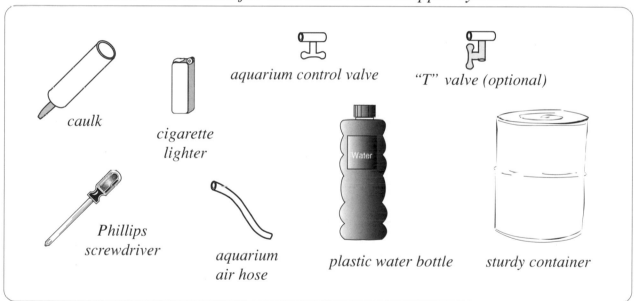

caulk

cigarette lighter

aquarium control valve "T" valve (optional)

Phillips screwdriver

aquarium air hose

Water

plastic water bottle sturdy container

*Materials needed for **each** Siphon dripper system*

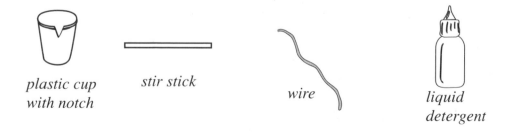

plastic cup with notch stir stick wire liquid detergent

© 1997 by The Regents of the University of California. LHS GEMS: *River Cutters.*

What You Need (for all sessions)

(List continued from page 8.)

Non-Consumables (continued)

- ❑ 5–8   trowels, sturdy spoons, or plastic putty knives
- ❑   collection of magazine pictures of the earth, and geology textbooks with photos of river features and geological landscapes
- ❑ 10   small containers or boxes (to hold event slips needed in Session 3)
- ❑ 1   overhead transparency of Earth today and 12,500 years ago (master on page 44)

Consumables

- ❑ 20   lbs. (9 kg) diatomaceous earth purchased from a swimming pool supply store or donated from a local high school or swim center
- ❑ 3+   bottles of blue food color, 1 oz. (30 ml), preferably in dropper bottles
- ❑ 1   bottle of red food color, 1 oz. (30 ml), in a dropper bottle
- ❑ 4   flexible plastic overlays or overhead transparencies, 8" x 10" (20 cm x 25 cm), for making dams (used or scratched transparencies work well)
- ❑ 32+   3" x 5" (8 cm x 13 cm) index cards for river feature flags
- ❑ 10–16   clear plastic straws
- ❑ 35   cotton swabs

Copies of the following:
- ❑ 32   copies of the Geological Features handout (master on pages 32–33)
- ❑ 32   copies of the Two River Valleys handout (master on page 65)
- ❑ 8   copies of Past Events data sheet (master on page 46)
- ❑ 32   copies of Timeline data sheet (master on page 45)

Optional:
- ❑ 1   bottle of yellow food color, 1 oz. (30 ml), in a dropper bottle
- ❑ 5–8   large garbage bags for covering the surfaces of the stacked tubs
- ❑ 5–8   envelopes or plastic bags to hold river feature flags

General Supplies

- ❑   plenty of water
- ❑   paper towels
- ❑ 1   watch/clock with second hand, clock preferred for Session 3
- ❑   overhead projector, transparencies, and markers (if no chalkboard is available)
- ❑   access to cooler or refrigerator (to store ice cubes for Session 3)
- ❑   a world map
- ❑ 5–8   pairs of scissors
- ❑ 160+   pieces of white paper
- ❑ 32   pencils

© 1997 by The Regents of the University of California. LHS GEMS: *River Cutters.*

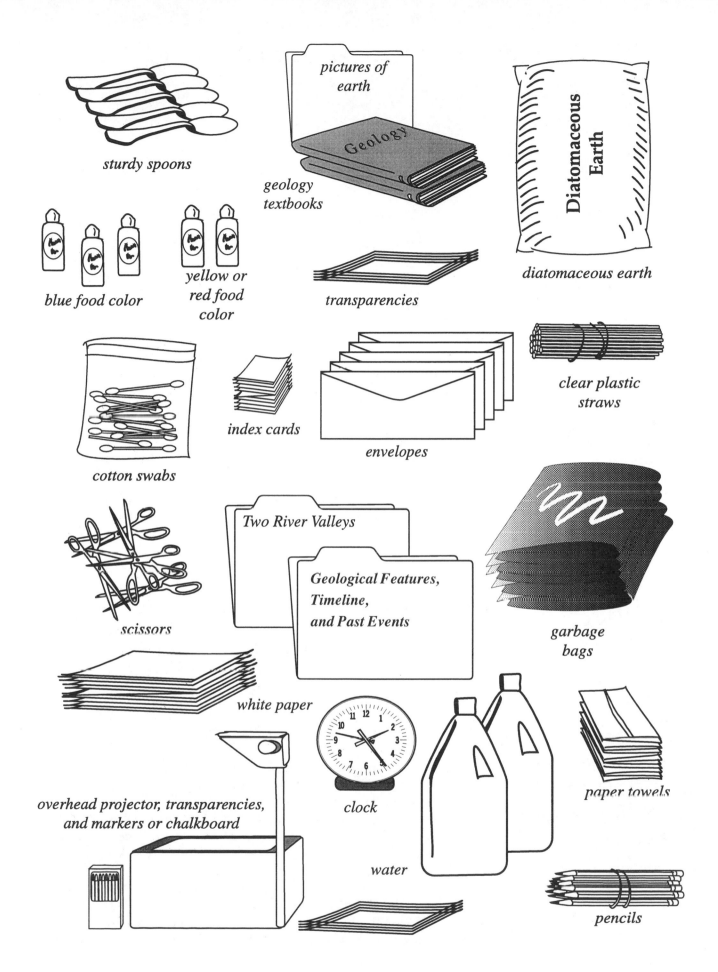

sturdy spoons

pictures of earth

geology textbooks

Geology

Diatomaceous Earth

diatomaceous earth

blue food color

yellow or red food color

transparencies

cotton swabs

index cards

envelopes

clear plastic straws

scissors

Two River Valleys

Geological Features, Timeline, and Past Events

garbage bags

white paper

clock

water

paper towels

overhead projector, transparencies, and markers or chalkboard

pencils

© 1997 by The Regents of the University of California. LHS GEMS: *River Cutters.*

Diatomaceous Earth Alert

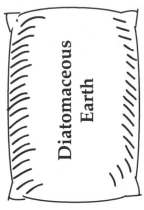

diatomaceous earth

Some pool supply stories use a volcanic ash known as perlite for filtration. This is not diatomaceous earth and will not work well in the river models.

IMPORTANT SAFETY NOTE

Diatomaceous earth is the substance used when students create their models of the formation of rivers. When mixed with the right proportion of water, diatomaceous earth works well to model river features, **if you have the right *kind* of diatomaceous earth, that is!**

The two most common commercial uses for diatomaceous earth are in swimming pool filtration and gardening. After it is mined, diatomaceous earth is milled to different textures for these two purposes. The particle size and texture you need to cut great rivers in *River Cutters* is the same as that needed for swimming pool filtration. **If you get your diatomaceous earth from a swimming pool supply store, it will work.** The swimming pool variety is bright white when dry and stays white when wet. (Some pool supply stores may label this substance "diatomite.")

The diatomaceous earth that does *not* work, sold in garden supply stores, is off-white or tan. When you add water, it turns brown, has a slimier texture, gets soupy easily, and water runs off it without cutting a channel. Color is not an absolute guarantee, however, as there may be special grades used in making paint that are white, but are not milled to the size and texture that works best for this activity.

VERY Best rule of thumb: Obtain only the diatomaceous earth used for swimming pool filtration!

Many pools use large quantities of diatomaceous earth, so they may be able to spare the amount you need for *River Cutters*. (There are some pools that don't use diatomaceous earth because they have a different type of filtration system.) If there is no source near you, this California corporation may be able to help or refer you to the appropriate regional outlet: Grefco Inc. (310) 517-0700.

Important Safety Note: It is necessary to wear a dust mask when you mix the dry diatomaceous earth with water and it's best to have good ventilation or do the mixing outside. Do not have students assist you. Contact lens wearers should either remove their lenses or put on safety glasses. Prolonged breathing of excessive concentrations of the dust can cause lung damage, or silicosis (there is silica in the diatomaceous earth) and bags of diatomaceous earth often include this warning. Since the diatomaceous earth is damp when used with students, dust should not be a problem in class.

Choosing and Making a River Flow System

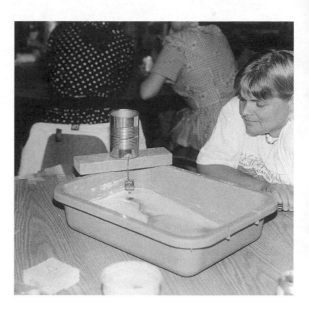

The simplest dripper system we've ever heard of uses a small styrofoam cup and a clothespin. A tiny hole is poked in the bottom of the cup, and attached to the side of the tub with the clothespin. The water drips out from the hole at the approximately correct rate. Kelly Vaughn, a teacher who recommended this method to us, says she used it successfully many times, adding that it is both easier and cheaper than other systems. On the other end of the spectrum, teachers have used high school laboratory equipment (a burette) to precisely control the drip rate, and we've even heard of teachers using unused, surplus medical IV equipment! Our experience has shown that most teachers prefer to use one of the following two systems:

(1) The "rain cloud" dripper system which requires some shopping and an hour or two to assemble a class set; but once constructed, rain cloud drippers can be reused for many years. These systems are quite easy for students to set up, and will save time during class. At this point in time, the rain cloud system is "state of the art" in *River Cutters* technology!

(2) The siphon dripper system that was featured in the original editions of this teacher's guide. The materials are inexpensive and the dripper cup sits directly on the diatomaceous earth, decreasing the chances of spills. However, students often require individual help in getting the siphon started and re-started, taking up class time. Also, the wire in the siphon will bend and rust making the equipment difficult to reuse, and some stores may no longer sell the two-holed stirrers. Both systems are described below. The choice is yours.

For *each* Rain Cloud dripper system you need:
- ❏ 1 plastic water bottle, 1 pt. to 1 qt. size
- ❏ silicone caulk (the type that remains flexible when dry) or a hot glue gun
- ❏ 1 piece of flexible aquarium air hose, 3"–5" long
- ❏ 1 adjustable plastic aquarium control valve
- ❏ 1 Phillips screwdriver (medium to large size—slightly smaller than diameter of the aquarium hose)
- ❏ 1 cigarette lighter, candle, or gas stove
- ❏ 1 metal coffee can, sturdy box, or plastic container to support the plastic bottle 8"–10" above the table (the piece of wood used to slope the earth can also be used)
- ❏ (*optional*) 1 "T" valve that fits onto the air hose, as an additional valve, to run two rivers at the same time.
- ❏ (*optional*) 1 additional adjustable aquarium control valve

Although some teachers have reported difficulty in finding aquarium control valves in their location, they are usually available in pet and/or aquarium stores. The inexpensive plastic valves are fine for these purposes. They are sometimes packaged in kits with, for example, five air control valves, four T-valves, and two suction cups. The plastic air control kit we obtained as we revised this guide cost about $3.00 and the tubing cost about $2.00.

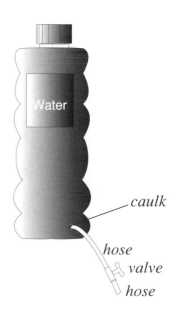

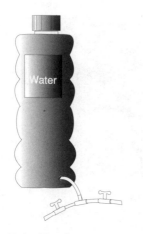

*Rain Cloud system
for two-river option*

1. In the side of the water bottle, approximately one half inch from the bottom, melt a hole with a Phillips screwdriver heated in the flame of a candle, cigarette lighter, or gas stove. The hole should be just large enough to accommodate the air hose.

2. Insert the air hose into the hole, and apply caulk on the outside, to seal the hole in the bottle. The caulk will need to dry at least 24 hours before use.

3. Add the control valve to the end of the hose, then attach another small piece of hose.

4. If you would like to make a system that will run two rivers concurrently, as well as separately, add a "T" valve, more hose, then a control valve near the end of each section of hose. Complete the system with two short pieces of hose.

5. Create a platform by upending the sturdy container, then position the dripper system above and at one end of a river-cutting tub. Make certain the control valve is closed before adding blue water to the bottle and testing the flow. Use the control valve to select a drip rate of approximately two drops per second. Let your first test drips drain into the pie pan.

For each Siphon dripper system you need:

❑ 1 wide-mouthed, tapered, soft plastic cup (9 oz.) with notch cut on edge
❑ 1 plastic stir stick with two small holes (commonly used as coffee stirrers)
❑ 1 piece of wire, 4" long (20 gauge or .035" in diameter), small enough to go through one hole in the stir stick
❑ 1 small squeeze bottle of liquid detergent

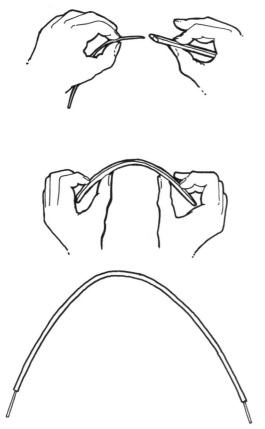

1. Insert the piece of wire into one of the two holes in a plastic stirrer.

2. Gently bend the stirrer with wire inside into a half-moon shape as shown. **Do not make any tight kinks in the stirrer as this will prevent water from flowing through it.** You can bend the stirrer around your forearm to avoid kinking it. Try to obtain a shape roughly similar to the illustration on this page.

3. Using scissors, cut a small notch in the edge of the plastic cup, as shown in the drawing. This will allow the dripper to rest in one place as it drips.

4. Prepare "river" water by adding 5–6 drops of blue food coloring to a 2-quart pitcher of water.

5. Add the blue water up to a point just below the notch on the cup. Also add one drop of detergent. The detergent helps keep air bubbles out of the dripper.

6. Place the cup on the upper end of the slope of diatomaceous earth midway between the two sides. Anchor the cup in the earth by pressing it down and turning it a few times so it sits firmly in the earth.

Testing the Siphon Dripper System

1. Fill a stirrer with water. To do this, insert the stirrer into the water cup, so both ends are under water, and the ends are oriented upward, as shown. You should see air bubbles coming out of one (or both) ends of the stirrer as the air leaves and the water enters. Gently slosh the stirrer up and down a few times until no more bubbles emerge.

2. When you think the stirrer is full of water, pick it up so the two ends remain upward. Then quickly invert it over the notch so one end is in the water and the other is over the earth.

3. If the stirrer begins dripping steadily, you have been successful. You may not succeed on the first try, or even the second, but once you have water in the stirrer, it will remain operational, even between uses, as long as the water does not flow out of it. If you want to remove it from the cup temporarily, rotate it sideways so it is in a horizontal position, rather than having one end lower than the other. Then the water should stay in it.

4. Adjust the flow rate to approximately thirty drops per 15 seconds (two drops per second) by bending the stirrer into slightly more of a "U" shape for a faster flow rate, or slightly less of a "U" shape for a slower flow rate.

5. As the water level of the cup lowers, it will need to be replenished. This can be done while the system is still in operation, but it should be done gently so as not to cause the stirrer to move too much, and not to cause bubbles to enter the dripper. Hold the dripper in place in its notch while you pour the water.

Whenever the stirrer is removed from the cup, it first should be rotated so it is level, then lifted and placed onto a flat surface. This allows the water to stay in it, making it ready for use again.

Getting Ready

Before the Day of the Activity

1. Begin to purchase and organize the equipment and materials at least a week or two in advance of the activity. A copy of the complete illustrated list of materials shown on pages 8–11 can be duplicated for volunteers who have agreed to assist you.

2. Do It Yourself First. Before you undertake this series of activities with your class, be sure to set up your own river-cutting tub to familiarize yourself with the materials and the river-cutting process. Start by reading this "Getting Ready" section and Session 1. This will help you demonstrate the use of the materials and gain a practical sense of the possibilities and limitations of the river models. Experience with setting up the tub will also help you decide how much of the preparation of the class materials can be done by your students. **(We recommend that students not assist in mixing the diatomaceous earth, and that it be done outside, using dust masks, and that other safety rules be observed.)**

3. Find out about how your local region was shaped by water. You can ask experts in your area, or figure it out for yourself from topographical maps of your community. (These are produced by the U.S. Geological Service and can be purchased in most cities or by mail.) By looking at contour lines, you will be able to identify erosion gullies, streams, and river valleys. Notice where these are located with respect to roads and buildings your students would know. If possible, find out approximately how long it took for these landforms to achieve their present shape. Think of some questions that will allow you to determine what your students believe about how these landforms may have been created. As described in "Behind the Scenes," the overall tilting of the landscape, which determines the direction a river flows, occurred over *millions of years*, while the shaping of most river valleys occurred over *many thousands of years*. However, it's also true that some river channels might shift overnight as a result of a single flood (see "The North Fork Is His Lab" on page 100).

4. Ask each student to bring in one or two magazine pictures of earth landscapes. Explain that the class will be investigating rivers. The pictures should show examples of how the surface of the earth has been shaped. You may want to mention that advertisements for cars, for example, frequently depict striking scenes of rugged mountain and desert terrain.

5. Choose one of the dripper systems (see pages 13–15). Make and assemble the appropriate number of systems for the number of teams in your class.

6. Prepare the river-cutting tubs.

Safety Note: (See note on page 12.) Wear a disposable dusk mask to prepare the tubs. The dust produced when working with diatomaceous earth can be irritating. If you wear contact lenses, remove them, or wear safety goggles, and follow these instructions:

a. Arrange the tubs side by side.

b. Fill a bucket with water and add 12 cups of water to each tub.

c. Put on your dust mask.

d. Open the bag of diatomaceous earth and use the measuring cup to add 13 cups of diatomaceous earth to each tub.

e. Using a trowel or sturdy spoon, stir the diatomaceous earth and water until all of the earth is wet. Depending on the humidity in your area you may need to add a little more earth or a little water in order to obtain good river-cutting action.

f. Remove the dust mask when the earth is wet.

g. Test the consistency by tilting the tub. Place a piece of wood under one edge, then slowly pour some water onto the earth. If the water soaks into the earth you need to mix more water into the earth before beginning the activity. If it runs off and forms a little gully, you have enough water.

h. Set the tubs aside for the day of the activity. If you want to stack the tubs, lay plastic garbage bags over the surfaces to prevent the wet earth from clinging to the bottoms of the tubs.

7. After each activity, the diatomaceous earth should remain in the tubs, so it can be used again. You can stack the tubs with plastic bags in between, as mentioned above.

8. Duplicate one copy of the Geological Features handout (for use in Sessions 2 and 3) for each student (masters on pages 32 and 33). Also duplicate one copy of the Two River Valleys handout (for use in Session 6) for each student (master on page 65).

The gray tubs we used in trial versions were standard rectangular trays used for bussing tables in restaurants. They measured 15" wide, 20" long, and 5" deep. Both the depth and length of the tub are important factors. Standard dishtubs are not large enough to yield adequate results. Restaurant supply stores, hardware, or paint stores are likely to carry plastic tubs of the proper dimensions.

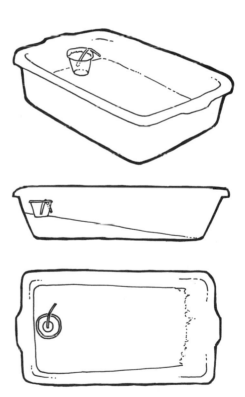

The Day of the Activity

1. Prepare blue water by adding 6–10 drops of blue food coloring to each of two pitchers of water. Keep the food coloring in a handy place in the event you need to replenish the supply of blue water.

2. Assemble the dripper systems and other materials in a manner that will be easy for students to retrieve. If you are using the rain cloud system, you can fill the water bottles with blue water before the activity, making sure that the caps are screwed on snugly and the dripper valves are closed.

3. River-Cutting Tubs Set-Up: Prepare the slope of the earth as described in the following steps. After you demonstrate this method, you can have your students do it for their team's river-cutting tubs.

> a. Position a wooden block under one end of the river-cutting tub, so the tub is elevated on one end.

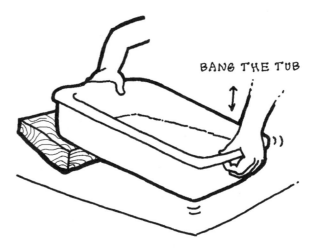

BANG THE TUB

> b. Press the end of the tub on the wooden block to hold it firmly, while you bang the other end of the tub up and down on the table to level the diatomaceous earth.

c. Remove the wooden block and place the tub flat on the table. The earth should form a uniform gentle slope.

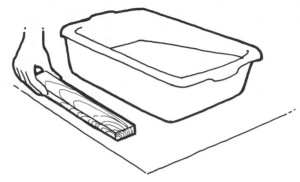

d. Let the tub rest for a minute while some water drains out. Sponge the surface to smooth the earth and soak up some of the water that will continue to collect at the bottom of the slope.

Note: This preparation step is extremely noisy if students are banging away at the same time. One teacher glues a strip of carpet padding onto the wooden block and bangs the tub on the block rather than on the table. You could also reduce classroom noise by having a volunteer help you to prepare the slopes in advance. Because water will continue to drain from the slopes, the surfaces will still need to be smoothed by students just prior to creating first rivers. If you transport the prepared slopes by car or on a cart, the motion will flatten the surfaces, and you will need to go through steps a.–d. again.

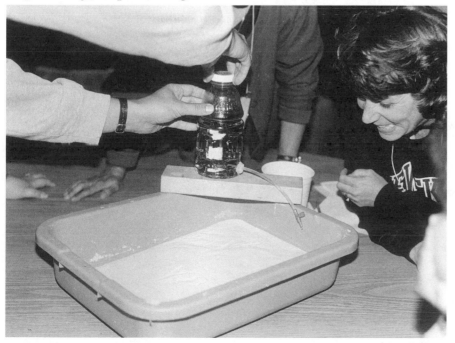

The Negro Speaks of Rivers
by Langston Hughes

I've known rivers:
I've known rivers ancient as the world and older than
     the flow of human blood in human veins.

My soul has grown deep like the rivers.

I bathed in the Euphrates when dawns were young.
I built my hut near the Congo and it lulled me to sleep.
I looked upon the Nile and raised the pyramids above it.
I heard the singing of the Mississippi when Abe Lincoln
     went down to New Orleans, and I've seen its
     muddy bosom turn all golden in the sunset.

I've known rivers:
Ancient, dusky rivers.

My soul has grown deep like the rivers.

From *Selected Poems* by Langston Hughes. Copyright 1926 by Alfred A. Knopf, Inc. and renewed 1954 by Langston Hughes. Reprinted by permission of the publisher.

Session 1: Exploring a Model River

Overview

The goal of the first session is for you to find out about your students' prior knowledge of river systems, and for your students to become familiar with their river models as a way to explore how rivers evolve. Begin by asking your students two or three key questions about how they think local landforms were created. Listen to their initial ideas and discuss some of the questions that river models may help them investigate. Then, demonstrate how to use the equipment and materials to create a river. Depending on your preference and the capabilities of your students, they may be more or less involved in preparing river-cutting tubs and drippers, but they should NOT be involved in mixing the diatomaceous earth.

The students are organized into teams and given the opportunity to acquaint themselves with the materials and model river systems, enjoyably developing useful techniques for future activities while exploring the potential of their models. Of special importance is helping students set up the dripper system so that it drips about two drops per second.

While students are creating their first trial rivers, you will have time to circulate among the teams encouraging them to describe and talk about what they see happening to the evolving rivers. This is a good time to learn more about your students' prior knowledge and vocabulary related to river features. Each team will show its river system to a partner team, thereby sharing and comparing observations and ideas among a larger group of students.

If you have a video showing bird's eye views of local geological features (see "America by Air" in the "Resources" section) you could start off the unit with a brief showing.

What You Need

For the class:
- ❑ 2 pitchers of blue-colored water
- ❑ 1 bottle of blue food coloring
- ❑ paper towels
- ❑ 1 bucket

For each team of 4–6 students:
- ❑ 1 river-cutting tub set-up (see instructions on pages 13–19)
- ❑ 1 sponge
- ❑ 1 piece of wood, 2" x 4" x 8"
- ❑ 1 aluminum pie pan
- ❑ 1 trowel or sturdy spoon

For each student:
- ❑ 1 piece of white paper
- ❑ pencil

Introducing River Cutter Models

1. Spend a few minutes asking your students how they think local landforms were created. For example, if the land is hilly, ask them what they think caused the hills to be shaped and located where they are. If the terrain is flat, ask the students why they think it is so flat. Reflect and paraphrase their ideas, encouraging discussion to reveal your students' ideas about forces that shape the land, particularly the role of water.

2. Ask the students questions, such as: "Has the land always looked like this?" "How might it have been different?" "If a valley (or other local landform) was not always here, how long do you think it took to form?" [If students say "thousands" or "millions" of years, ask them to explain what they mean by those large numbers. Were people alive thousands of years ago? Millions of years ago?] Ask, "Do you think the land around us might be changing today?" "What might change it?" "Do you know of any other landforms that were shaped by water?" "What are they?"

3. Explain that scientists often use models to investigate processes that are difficult to observe directly. Let them know that in this unit they will use models to investigate the role of water in shaping the land. In particular, they will investigate answers to questions, such as:
- How was our local landscape shaped by water?
- What makes some river valleys deep and others shallow?
- How long does it take for a river valley to form and how does it change over time?
- What are the different features of river systems?
- What happens if a river is dammed up?
- How does groundwater pollution affect river systems?

It is not difficult for students to visualize how a river shapes the land if they live where a river, creek, or lake runs through the town (as in Willamette, Oregon, pictured above). But even regions that have no bodies of water today have probably been shaped by flowing water. For example, many areas that are large, flat expanses were once the floor of an ocean or lake, where sediment accumulated over millions of years.

Photo by G. Donald Bain, University of California at Berkeley

4. Emphasize that model rivers make it possible to speed up time to see how river systems change over many thousands and even millions of years, so that we can see what will happen over many human generations in just a few minutes.

5. Show the students the river-cutting tub and the dripper system. Explain that the tub contains a mixture of water with a substance called *diatomaceous earth*. This "earth" is made up of the shell-like skeletons of tiny plants called *diatoms* that accumulated on the bottom of seas millions of years ago. (You may want to show the students the micrograph of a diatom on page 76). Explain that in their model, the diatomaceous earth represents the land.

6. Point out the dripper system and show the students how it works. Ask the students what they think it may represent in their model. Encourage them to describe a variety of possibilities, such as a rainstorm, waterfall, or flood. Tell the students that they will use their models to find out more about what happens when a river is cut naturally into the earth. They will be working in teams to carefully observe what happens to all parts of the river as it is formed. In today's session, they will explore the equipment and materials and make their first rivers.

Demonstrating How to Make a River

1. Use one of the river-cutting tubs as a demonstration tub for the students. The earth inside the tub should be sloped, and the tub should be level with no piece of wood under it.

2. Demonstrate how to set up the dripper system, letting it drip a minute or so. Show the students how to adjust the drip rate to about 2 drips/second.

3. Invite students to imagine that the tub is a miniature landscape and that they themselves are tiny. Orient them to the small scale of the model with questions that might stimulate them to use their prior knowledge of rivers such as: "If you were even smaller than a tiny ant, what features might you expect to see while walking along the banks of our tiny model river?" "What do you predict you might encounter during a raft trip down this miniature river?"

4. Stop your sample river, and demonstrate how to use the piece of wood to re-slope the earth in the tub. Tell them that if the ground does not level completely, to try banging the tub a little harder.

5. If the drippers are not already full, appoint a volunteer who will help you circulate among the teams, pouring blue water from a pitcher into the drippers.

6. Tell teams that when they receive their materials, one half of each team should prepare the tubs by sloping the earth, while the other half of each team tests the dripper system and sets the drip rate by letting the system drip into a pie pan.

Students Prepare River Models

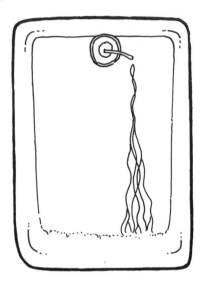

1. Organize teams of 4–6 students each and arrange the desks or other tables in your classroom so that each river cutter model is on a flat surface. Ask a member of each team to obtain the river-cutting tubs and dripper systems from the distribution stations.

2. Encourage students to pick up a little bit of diatomaceous earth and examine it to satisfy their curiosity; but tell them **not** to touch the earth after starting their rivers.

3. Circulate among the groups, helping them to set up their river models, answering questions, and making sure that all members of a team are getting a chance to interact with the materials and equipment.

Students Create Their First River Models

1. Refocus the attention of the entire class, providing any additional pointers you think may be needed, and tell the teams to start their river models by letting the water drip for five minutes. This five-minute period represents 5,000 years in the life of a river. Tell them you want them to describe and talk with each other about what they see happening during the five-minute period.

2. Caution the students not to try to alter the course of the river during the experiment. **The whole idea of using this model is to find out what happens as a river is cut naturally into the earth.** While the river is running they should **not touch the tub or dripper system**—but they should watch closely to see what is happening.

3. Circulate around the class again, answering any questions that may arise, checking the drip rates, and making a mental note of the vocabulary and ideas students are expressing. Encourage them to describe what is happening to the water and the earth.

4. When teams complete the five-minute rivers, tell them to stop the drippers. Hand out a piece of white paper to each student and have them draw the rivers they have created. Ask them to label features and write notes about anything special that they observed.

5. Direct pairs of teams to share their experiences and river systems with each other, discussing the events and features they observed. Ask them to share what they learned about how water shapes the land from this activity.

6. If the discussion (Session 2) is to immediately follow the lab period, **tell students to keep their practice rivers intact.**

7. If the discussion period will not follow immediately after the lab, demonstrate cleanup procedures. Show the students how to remove the "ocean" that has formed at one end of the tub by using the sponge to soak up the water and squeeze it into the pie pan.

8. Designate a volunteer to visit each team with a bucket to receive the water collected in the pie pans. Explain that the water cannot be poured down the drain until the diatomaceous earth has settled to the bottom. Then the clear water may be used to water the garden or decanted into the sink.

9. The tubs can be left in place if they will be used again by another class, or they can be stacked at the side of the room, with plastic garbage bags between each tray so they do not stick.

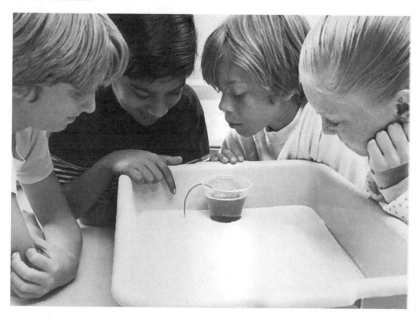

Session 2: Discussing River Features

Overview

In this session, your students increase their knowledge of river features by discussing the rivers they created in the last session, and comparing their model rivers with local geological features. They then compare their models with photos and diagrams showing a variety of river features. The discussion should be appropriate for the age level of your students and their prior experiences with earth science. Concentrate on what your students actually observed in their models and solicit their prior knowledge of river systems.

After discussing the features of their model rivers, you will build on your students' observations by introducing the processes of erosion and weathering that tear down landforms, and processes that build up landforms, such as deposition, volcanism, and uplift. Lastly the students make marker flags, for use in the fourth session.

What You Need

For the class:
- ❑ overhead projector transparencies and pens, or chalkboard and chalk, or butcher paper

For each team of 4–6 students:
- ❑ at least 4 blank 3" x 5" index cards
- ❑ 1 pencil
- ❑ 1 pair of scissors
- ❑ collection of earth photographs and/or geology textbooks with photos of river features and geological landscapes, such as canyons, snow-covered mountains, eroded deserts, coastlines, volcanoes, and fossils in sedimentary layers.
- ❑ (optional) 1 envelope or plastic bag to hold the river feature flags

Instead of index cards, you could also use cut up pieces of overhead transparency material for the river feature flags. Students can write on these with indelible pens. This is an excellent use of scratched transparencies.

For each student:
- ❑ 1 copy of the Geological Features handout (master on pages 32, 33)

Getting Ready

Before the Day of the Activity

1. Ask students to bring in magazine pictures of landscapes and geological features.

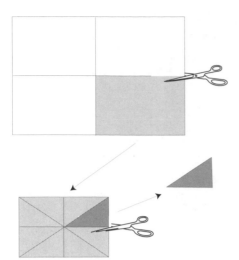

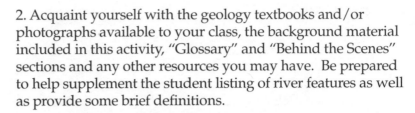

2. Acquaint yourself with the geology textbooks and/or photographs available to your class, the background material included in this activity, "Glossary" and "Behind the Scenes" sections and any other resources you may have. Be prepared to help supplement the student listing of river features as well as provide some brief definitions.

3. As described on page 16, learn as much as you can about how local geological landforms were shaped by water and about how long it took for these to form.

The Day of the Activity

Assemble the materials for making the river feature flags. Be prepared to demonstrate how to cut a 3" x 5" index card into four equal rectangles, then to cut the rectangles into eight equal triangles.

Discussing River Features

1. Tell the students that today they will discuss the results of their first river cutting session, starting with identification of river features. Later they will discuss *how* the water created the features.

2. Ask them to imagine once again they are tiny travelers—what features did they see along the model rivers? Encourage students to tell you about different formations or river features they observed in their river-cutting tubs, and list their responses on the chalkboard or butcher paper, as the start of an ongoing list of river-related and geological features that will remain in the classroom throughout the unit.

3. The model river enables the students to view the entire watershed and gain a sense of the factors that influence the direction of flow. Ask questions to stimulate their thinking, such as: "If you couldn't see where the water is dripping from, how would you know which way the water is flowing?" "What seems to influence the course that the river takes?"

4. Ask the students if any of the features they observed in their tubs reminded them of any real geological features in their community, or that they have seen before. Allow time for students to discuss their observations.

5. Add any information you may have learned about how local landforms were shaped by water over thousands of years. Share any photos, maps, or information from experts where you may have gained insights.

Geological features caused by water include:

- *islands*
- *sand bars*
- *deltas*
- *valleys*
- *mudflows*
- *lakes*
- *caves*
- *rapids*
- *channels*
- *forks*
- *tributaries*

6. Distribute a copy of both pages of the Geological Features handout (master on pages 32–33) to each student, as well as pictures and textbooks containing photographs or illustrations of river systems. Have students work in pairs or small groups to review the materials with the goal of identifying as many features as they can that might appear in their model rivers.

7. Reconvene the class and ask them to add to the list any new features that they saw in the resource materials that they also observed in their models.

8. During the discussion, if the terms have not already surfaced, you may want to add that the place where a stream starts is called the *source*, and that smaller streams which flow into a larger river are called *tributaries*. A river with all of its connecting tributaries and streams is called a *river system.*

9. Ask the students, "Did you ever see any of these features along a real river or creek?" "Are there any features of a real river that you have **not** yet seen in the models?" (Encourage any comments that suggest the students are making connections between their models and the real world. Erosion gullies or places where streams flow across the beach on their way to the ocean are good examples.)

Processes that Tear Down Land Forms

1. Ask the students, "What happens to the diatomaceous earth that is pushed out of the way when the water cuts a river in your models?" They will probably notice that the material is moved downstream by the water.

2. Define the word erosion. Some students may already be familiar with the concept. A definition of *erosion* is the wearing away of land by water, waves, wind, or glaciers. In the case of rivers, erosion is the moving of material by water. Explain that wherever water flows over soil or rock, erosion is taking place.

3. Ask the students, "Can anyone give me an example of erosion near our school or near your home?" Take several responses. If students do not mention it, point out that erosion can often be seen after a series of rainstorms, when the soil can't soak up any more water. They will see tiny streams of water run through the soil. As these streams run, they become muddy because they pick up small particles of dirt and rock. Over thousands of years, entire hillsides will eventually wind up on the bottom of a lake or ocean.

4. Point out that the model contains a soft, powdery material, but the real world contains mountains of hard rock in addition to soft soil. Over thousands of years, hard rock is broken down into soil as it is warmed and cooled by the sun each day, and slowly dissolved by acid rain. The breaking down of rock into soil is called *weathering*.

Drainage patterns can be another interesting and related discussion topic. Explain that streams and rivers produce a variety of drainage patterns, depending in part on the features of the land through which they flow. Ask, "What kind of drainage pattern might occur on a flat area, as compared to a mountainous region?" Encourage all responses. Remind students that by actually changing the shape of the land through erosion, rivers also change the drainage patterns. For example, on more level land, streams or rivers tend to create S-shaped bends, called meanders. As the land is worn down, one bend may meet another to form a lake, perhaps a long curved-type lake called an oxbow lake. In connection with large scale movements of the earth and over time, a river may cut deep valleys through the earth, or create terraces, gorges, or canyons.

Stream channel worn through solid rock

photo by Lisa Wells, Vanderbilt University

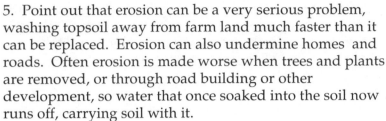

5. Point out that erosion can be a very serious problem, washing topsoil away from farm land much faster than it can be replaced. Erosion can also undermine homes and roads. Often erosion is made worse when trees and plants are removed, or through road building or other development, so water that once soaked into the soil now runs off, carrying soil with it.

Processes that Build Up Land Forms

1. Explain that the material carried by water is called *sediment*. Ask the students, "What happens to the sediment carried by your model rivers?" [They will probably see that it is deposited further downstream.] Some of it winds up in the form of a delta, where their rivers enter a lake or the ocean. (Sediment is also deposited on floodplains and alluvial fans.) Explain that this process, which also occurs in the real world, is called *deposition*. The processes of weathering and erosion wear away high landforms, while deposition builds up new landforms in low areas.

You may want to ask students for their ideas on how much sediment a slowly-moving river carries, as opposed to one that moves quickly. They may want to observe their river models for ideas on this question, and/or design an experiment in later sessions.

2. Ask the students, "What would happen to all of the mountains and hills in the world if weathering, erosion, and deposition were the only forces shaping the land?" [They will probably infer that after a few million years, all mountains and hills would eventually be flattened by erosion, and the sedimentary material would be deposited in lakes and oceans, thus leveling the entire planet.] Ask, "Is there any evidence in your model that supports your prediction?" [Material is washed down the slope into the "sea." In time the slope will be gone and all high places will be eroded.] "Why does that NOT happen?

Based on various factors, rivers deposit more or less of the materials they are carrying. When a stream flows into a lake or ocean, it deposits material as it enters the larger body of water. These deposits are deltas. Or, in a mountain desert region, in a place where there are normally no rivers, a spring "flash flood" may surge out of a mountain gorge, spread out, and, as the water dries, deposit the material it was carrying in a large fan-shaped area called an alluvial fan.

3. Ask, "Why is the Earth not levelled?" "How come we still have mountains and hills?" Invite several responses, asking the students to describe some of the processes that build up the land, such as volcanoes, uplift of continents, and mountain-building. If students do not know about these processes you can describe them briefly. *(Note: If older students have been introduced to the theory of plate tectonics, you may allude to it here. Otherwise it is sufficient to explain that the Earth's crust is always in motion.)*

4. Point out that if we could speed up time—so that one thousand years passed in just one minute—we could see how "constructive" forces (such as volcanism, uplift, and deposition) built up the land, and how "destructive forces" (such as erosion and weathering) wore it down. That's what our models do for us—allow us to see what would happen to the river system if we could speed up time.

What Do Models Tell Us?

1. Remind the students about some of the ideas they expressed at the beginning of the first session concerning how landforms are created. Ask them: "Do you now believe that your earlier ideas were correct?" "If you do, how did the models support your theories?" "If you have changed your minds, how did the models help you see things in a different way?"

2. Ask the students to explain some of the ways that their river models are like the real world, and ways that they are different.

3. Ask your students to reflect on the advantages and disadvantages of using models in science with questions such as:

*   Keeping in mind that models are somewhat like the real world—but not exactly like it—how can models help us understand processes like the formation of landforms? [They enable us to explore in the laboratory processes that would take thousands of years to observe in nature. They also show us the entire river system, from source to delta, and everything in between.]

*   In what ways should we be careful in using models to understand natural processes? [Since models are not exactly like the real world, we could reach the wrong conclusions if we depended on models alone.]

Making River Features Flags

1. Explain to the students that later in the unit they will keep more careful track of what the model rivers are doing to the earth over time, and that one way to do this is to make small flags with names of river features that they can plant in the earth whenever one of these features appears.

2. Demonstrate how to cut a 3" x 5" index card into four equal rectangles, then cut the rectangles into eight equal triangles (see illustration on page 28). Label one end of a triangle with a river feature such as "rapids."

3. Have the students organize themselves into the same teams as in Session 1 and provide each team with about four index cards, a pencil, and a pair of scissors. Direct them to cut the cards into triangles, then prepare a set of river labels they think will occur during river runs. You may want to place the river feature flags from each team in plastic bags or envelopes.

Geological Features

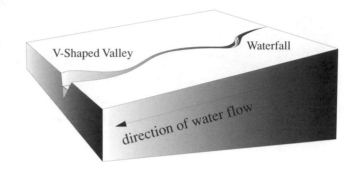

The river in the photo above has formed a *valley with a V-shaped profile.* Many rivers in V-shaped valleys have rapids and waterfalls.

Above is a diagram of a *V-shaped valley.* The arrow shows which way the water is flowing.

The river in the photo at left flows through narrow *channels* in a shallow valley. The *floodplain* is the flat area that borders the river, which is covered with water in times of flooding. Sediment deposited on the floodplain probably comes from the mountains in the distance that show erosion *gullies* and *canyons.*

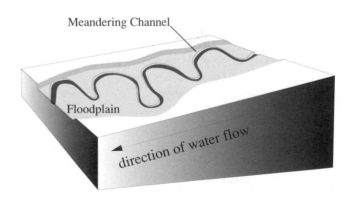

A rounded, or "S"-shaped bend or loop is called a *meander.* The river in the photo above flows in a meandering channel within a very wide, shallow valley. The valley floor is a large floodplain which is now rich farm land.

Above is a diagram of a wide, shallow valley. A *meandering channel* winds through the floodplain.

©1997 by the Regents of the University of California. LHS GEMS: *River Cutters.*
May be duplicated for classroom or workshop use.

Geological Features (continued)

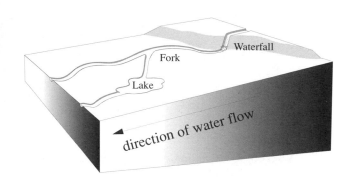

Waterfalls, like the one in the above photo, occur where the land through which a river flows drops rapidly. Some rivers, like the one shown in the diagram above and to the right, start out flowing rapidly in mountainous areas, then gradually slow when they reach shallower slopes, finally forming deltas when they reach the ocean. (The photo and diagram at the bottom of this page show deltas.)

An *alluvial fan* is a deposit of sediment that forms where a fast-flowing stream reaches more level land, spreads out, and is absorbed or evaporates. The small alluvial fans pictured to the left were deposited on sand dunes.

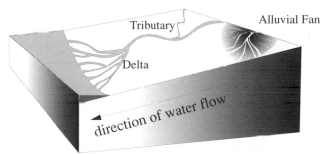

This diagram above shows an alluvial fan, a delta, and a *tributary*, which is a river that joins a larger river.

A *delta* is a deposit of sediment that occurs where a river or stream flows into a larger body of water. Deltas can be small, like the one pictured to the left, or large enough for entire cities to be built on them.

©1997 by the Regents of the University of California. LHS GEMS: *River Cutters.*
May be duplicated for classroom or workshop use.

The above photo shows Niagara Falls, which is on the border of the United States and Canada. The falls started a long time ago in a place where the river flowed over a tall cliff. Since that time Niagara Falls has "moved" 7 miles upstream, leaving a deep gorge. This has occurred because the river bottom consists of hard rock over a layer of soft rock. Wearing away the soft rock undermines the hard rock until it falls in chunks. Between 1850 and 1950, the Falls moved 400 feet upstream. How far did it move in one year? [4 feet/year]. If the rate has stayed about the same, how long has it taken for the falls to "move" 7 miles to its present location? [5,280 feet/mile x 7 miles = 36,960 feet. 36,960 feet/4 feet per year = 9,240 years.]

Session 3: Time and the River

Overview

In the previous sessions, the students had the opportunity to familiarize themselves with the materials, and begin observing how rivers carve the land. Because this model condenses time, students may acquire an erroneous perception that these changes occur quickly.

This activity is designed to help your students understand the difficult concept of "deep time," to gain a more accurate sense of how long the river features in their model might take to form in actual rivers. Although some changes in a river may occur quickly, as a result of a large storm or earthquake, most river features evolve through gradual erosion and the accumulated effects of many storms over thousands of years. And the geological conditions and large landforms that provide the framework for the formation of the rivers we know today have of course developed over many millions of years.

What You Need

For the class:
- ❏ river model equipment from Session 1 and 2
- ❏ 10 small containers for distribution of historical event slips: (strawberry baskets, small boxes, file folders, envelopes, etc.).
- ❏ large clock with second hand
- ❏ cooler or refrigerator to store ice cubes before use
- ❏ overhead transparency of Earth now and 12,000 years ago (master on page 44)
- ❏ world map

For each team of 2-4 students:
- ❏ 1 ice cube
- ❏ 1 copy of Past Events data sheet, page 46

For each student:
- ❏ 1 sheet of blank paper for drawing rivers
- ❏ 1 pencil
- ❏ 1 copy of the Timeline data sheet, page 45

Getting Ready

1. Label the containers with large numbers: #1 through #10.

2. Make one copy for each team of the Past Events sheet, page 46. Cut out each event from the historical event sheet, and place them in the appropriate labeled containers.

Some teachers may prefer, rather than cutting out the events and having students get up and obtain them, to provide teams with a sheet folded up from the bottom, event by event. Students can then unfold the paper from the top, event by event, as you call out the time. On page 47 we provide a timeline listing which could be copied and used in this way.

3. Make overhead transparencies of page 44 showing the Earth today and during the last ice age.

4. Prepare a Timeline on the chalkboard, like the Timeline data sheet on page 45. Do this by drawing a vertical line, 1.2 meters tall. Make a tick mark every 10 centimeters. Label the line and place numbers as shown in the Timeline data sheet. These numbers correspond to those on the Past Events sheet. You will add titles next to the numbers during the activity.

#1	12,000 years ago, Ice Age Ends
#2	8,000 years ago, Ice Has Melted
#3	3,000 years ago, Olmec Civilization
#4	2,500 years ago, Great Pyramid
#5	2,200 years ago, Great Wall of China
#6	2,000 years ago, Roman Empire
#7	1,000 years ago, Empire of Ancient Ghana
#8	500 years ago, Columbus Sails
#9	225 years ago, United States Established
#10	30 years ago, First Landing on the Moon

Important Note on Timing: It is essential that students have at least **12 minutes** to conduct the Timeline Activity, plus time to discuss and clean up. Try to move quickly through the first two parts: Setting the Scene and Carving Glacial Valleys, so there will be time to finish the activity in one period.

Setting the Scene: The Ice Age

1. Tell student teams to set up their river systems, starting the dripper at approximately 2 drops per second. Allow them to continue to either carve the same river canyons from Session 2, or have them start a new river canyon.

2. When all the systems are up and dripping, gather the students away from the tubs where they can watch a large clock with a second hand. Tell them that geological time is so vast that it's difficult to comprehend. To get an idea of geological time, they are going to use a model that will condense time, so they can watch it "fly by."

3. Explain that in this model, **one minute will represent 1,000 years.** So, it will take **12 minutes to simulate the last 12,000 years** of Earth history. At this scale, one second is about 17 years. Ask the students, "On this scale, how long ago were you born?" [Less than a second for any student under 17.] Ask the students to watch the clock tick off seconds, and to think about each second representing the lifetime of a teenager. Ask them how long 100 years would be [6 seconds] How long would 500 years be? [30 seconds]

4. Ask your students: "What do you think the Earth was like 12,000 years ago?" [Allow some time for responses.]

5. Show the overhead transparency comparing the Earth of today with the Earth of 12,000 years ago, while you explain what Earth was like at that time:

12,000 years ago it was much colder than today. Today we call that period an "Ice Age." Thirty percent of the world's land area was covered with ice. Almost all of Canada, the northern third of the U.S., much of Europe and eastern Siberia, and all of Scandinavia were covered with ice. The area that is now New York City was covered by ice and snow—**two miles deep!** Seattle was covered three miles deep!

Thick layers of ice and snow are called *glaciers.* As you might imagine, glaciers are very heavy. Where the land is not perfectly level, they slowly slide downhill, cutting and carving deep valleys.

Because so much water was frozen up in the ice, the oceans at that time were lower and **more land was exposed.** When glaciation was at its peak there were more land bridges between continents, including one between Alaska and Siberia.

Many human artifacts in North America date from about 12,000 years ago, and some anthropologists and archaeologists believe that large numbers of the earliest Americans came across this "land bridge" from Asia during that time, following animals who migrated across the land bridge, which could have been as much as 1000 miles wide!

Huge mammals adapted for cold weather roamed the northern areas, including 13-foot-tall woolly mammoths, 20-foot-tall giant ground sloths, 15-foot-long armadillos, woolly rhinoceros, saber-toothed cats, mastodons, giant bison, horses, yaks, wolves, and musk oxen.

Note: Exactly when the first peoples inhabited the American continents remains an open question. New findings keep moving the date back. While the "land bridge" of 12,000 years ago probably led to an increase in migration, there is also evidence dated at more than 17,000 years ago, and some sources estimate back to 50,000 B.C. and even earlier! It is thought that the land bridge came and went as the Ice Ages fluctuated, and earlier migrations thus very likely. There are also theories about people who sailed from the South Seas or other parts of Asia and about ancient African voyagers who may have reached the Americas. Deeply-rooted Native American traditions suggest that people have lived in the Americas for much longer than science has been able to confirm. A comment by Jack Weatherford may be to the point: "Columbus arrived in the New World in 1492, but America has yet to be discovered." The background section of the GEMS guide Investigating Artifacts *contains some related information on Native American origins and other issues.*

Carving Glacial Valleys

1. Explain that many rivers in North America run through valleys that were once formed by glaciers. Tell your students that each team will simulate this using an ice cube to represent a glacier.

2. Use a river model tub to demonstrate the formation of a glacial valley. Stop the dripper, then push the ice cube down into the diatomaceous earth, perpendicular to the river canyon, near where the river begins. Push the ice cube so it sinks part way into the earth, then slowly push it towards the bottom of the tub, carving out a long valley by pushing the diatomaceous earth in front of it. Tell them not to make the valley too deep, and not to further alter the landscape (other than allowing the dripper to run). Point out that real glaciers moved very slowly, from a few inches to a few feet per year.

3. Tell the students that when they receive their ice cube they will:

    a. Stop their drippers.

    b. Use the cube to carve a glacial valley.

    c. At your signal, start a river running through the valley, at about 2 drips/second.

    d. Let the river run for about 500 years (30 seconds in the time scheme of the model where 1 second equals about 17 years).

4. Explain that you'd like them to pause after they've carved the glacial valley until all teams have finished carving, so they can all start the 30-second river run together.

5. Distribute the ice cubes, and send the students back to their river models to begin their glacial activity. When all of the groups have carved a glacial valley, announce the beginning and end of a 30 second/500 year period. At the end of the 30 seconds, tell your students to stop their drippers.

6. After the 30 second/500 year run, hand out a sheet of blank paper to each student. Have them draw how their rivers look at this stage.

7. Point out one major difference between glacial valleys and river valleys—glacial valleys tend to be more U-shaped, while river valleys, tend to be more V-shaped. Explain that many rivers in North America were originally glacial valleys that rivers later began to run through, just as they modeled in this activity.

You could ask students if any of the groups observed a "bay" form as their glacial valleys were flooded by rising waters. Explain that many bays were created this way, including San Francisco Bay. The Great Lakes were also carved by glaciers, then flooded by rising waters.

Introducing the 12,000 Year Timeline

1. Gather the students away from the tubs and ask them:

- What happened as the river valley carved through the glacial valleys? [The new river probably flowed through the wide valley, cutting a new channel.]

- How did the rivers change over 500 years? [Answers will vary.]

- How much do you think a river will change in a single human lifetime, of less than 100 years?" [Be open to students' various ideas.]

2. Tell the students that in the next activity, they're going to model 12,000 years —more than 120 lifetimes! Ask them to predict what kind of changes they think might occur in a 12-minute run (12,000 years).

3. Remind them that when they start off at 12,000 years ago, they will be in an Ice Age, when much of North America (and other parts of the world) was covered with ice, and the land was slowly being carved by huge glaciers.

4. Hand out a Timeline data sheet to each student. Tell them that you will announce the passage of important historical events. Point out the numbered containers. Explain that the moment you say the number of an event, they should send one member of their team to get a slip of paper describing the event and when it occurred. They are to then write the title of the event in the appropriate spot on their timeline.

Depending on the experience of your students, you may choose to review the historical events included in the timeline, before beginning the activity. If you have many students for whom English is a second language, you may choose to have them draw pictures for each event on their timeline.

Note: The Olmec culture is one of the most fascinating cultures of ancient Mexico. Olmec culture is considered the "mother culture" of civilization in Mesoamerica. The Olmecs developed advanced agricultural systems, domesticated animals. built ceremonial centers, and created sculptures and huge carved stone monuments of great beauty and unique style. Their art and monuments have come down to the present, but much remains unknown about their origins and decline. It is estimated that the ascendance of Olmec civilization took place between 1300 B.C, and 600 B.C., with some sources going back even further to from 1500 B.C. to 1200 B.C. Given these ranges, we've chosen 3000 years ago as an estimated time line location.

5. Tell the students to describe any significant changes they observe in their valleys on the appropriate spot on their timeline.

6. Send the groups back to their tubs and start the 12-minute period. As each minute passes, announce that 1,000 years have just passed. Fill out your own 12,000 year timeline on the chalkboard.

7. For much of the first part of the 12-minute run, there are few historical events, so your students will have a chance to carefully observe their rivers and others. You may wish to ask one student from each team to remain standing by their river tub and encourage other students to observe their own river carefully but also walk around the room to compare what is happening in the other rivers.

8. Following is the time schedule and announcements that you will make during the 12-minute run.

> **Start!** (12,000 years ago)
> #1 Ice age ends. Increase the flow rate to five drops per second.
>
> **4 minutes** (8,000 years ago)
> #2 Ice has melted. Reduce the flow rate to two drops per second.
>
> **9 minutes** (3000 years ago)
> #3 Olmec Civilization.
>
> **9 minutes, 30 seconds** (2,500 years ago)
> #4 Great Pyramid in Egypt.
>
> **9 minutes, 50 seconds** (2,200 years ago)
> #5 Great Wall of China.
>
> **10 minutes** (2,000 years ago)
> #6 Roman Empire.
>
> **11 minutes** (1,000 years ago)
> #7 Empire of Ancient Ghana.
>
> **11 minutes, 30 seconds** (500 years ago)
> #8 Columbus sets sail.
>
> **11 minutes, 45 seconds** (225 years ago)
> #9 United States established.
>
> **11 minutes, 58 seconds** (30 years ago)
> #10 People land on the Moon.
>
> **12 minutes: Stop!**

Discussion

1. Assemble your students away from the materials to discuss the activity. Ask the students to reflect on the timescale: "In our model, how long ago was ...

... The Olmec Civilization?"   [180 seconds, 3,000 years ago]

... The Roman Empire?"   [120 seconds, 2,000 years ago]

... Columbus' Voyage?"   [30 seconds, or 500 years ago]

... Establishment of the U.S.?"   [15 seconds, or 225 years ago]

... The first landing on the moon?"   [2 seconds, or 30 years ago]

... The date of your birth?"   [less than 1 second ago]

2. Ask students to describe how their rivers changed over long periods of time (thousands of years), and over shorter periods, comparable to the lifetime of a person (less than 100 years). Ask them about changes in the "sea level," where their rivers empty into a pool at the bottom of the tub, as well as changes in the river channel, delta, and so on. [Responses will vary, but in general, they may infer that rivers change very little in a person's lifetime, and quite a bit over thousands of years.]

3. Show the class the photo of Niagara Falls on page 34, and read the caption. Ask the students how Niagara Falls might have appeared to be different if their great grandparents had gone to see it, 100 years ago. [The water must have been falling 4 feet x 100 = 400 feet further downstream—a little more than the length of a football field.] This illustrates that it is hard for a person to directly observe these kinds of changes in a river—because they take time. It's very unlikely that they would happen to be there at exactly the time, for example, that a large piece of rock fell—if they were, then in that case they would see a fairly major change in a short time.

4. Extend the students' understanding of deep time by explaining that the period of time modeled in this lesson—12,000 years—is really just the most recent phase of the Earth's long history. For example:

- The Ice Ages began about 2 million years ago. During that time, the Earth has cooled and warmed about 18 times. If we ran our rivers using the same scale of 1 minute = 1,000 years, it would take about **33 hours** to model the 2 million year period and represent in the models how much the land would change as the glaciers formed and melted again and again.

- Long before the Ice Ages, dinosaurs inhabited the Earth, then became extinct 65 million years ago. We would have to run our model 45 days to model how much the land might change since the dinosaurs became extinct!

5. Conclude by asking the students:

- How did you learn from today's activity about the way water shapes land forms? [Glaciers and rain have helped to create river systems. Rivers are always changing, but very slowly.]

- What did you learn about how long it takes for river systems to form? [Answers will vary. Look for innovative ways to express very long periods of time.] Encourage students to keep the timescale they've just experienced in mind as they take part in the other sessions in this unit.

- What is the oldest structure in your area? City Hall? Local hills? Local rivers? [Geological "structures" are many, many times older than buildings!]

- Why are models helpful for studying natural processes like the formation of river systems? [Answers will vary. If students do not mention it, emphasize that without models it is difficult for people—with our life spans—to notice changes that take place over very long periods of time.]

Going Further

1. Tell your students that when they were making the "tilt" in the tubs at the beginning of the activity, it represented the uplifting of mountains, such as the Rockies 70 million years ago. The Allegheny mountains, which cause rivers from the Eastern mountains to flow into the Mississippi, were pushed upwards starting about 450 million years ago—even before the dinosaurs. Challenge the students to figure out how much time they would have to run their models to represent the time since the Allegheny mountains rose, 450 million years ago. [312 days, or almost a year].

2. While the time scale of 1 minute = 1,000 years is helpful for some students, others can more easily grasp long periods of time by using distances to represent time. Give your students the scale of 1 meter = 10,000 years and have them create a timeline showing the ten events from the Past Events data sheet. Then, have them figure out how long their timeline should be to show the following events at the same scale:

Beginning of the Ice Ages	2 million years ago
Extinction of the Dinosaurs	65 million years ago
Rise of Appalachian Mountains	450 million years ago
Formation of the Earth	4,500 million years ago

[At this scale, in order to show the beginning of the Ice Ages, the students would need a timeline 200 meters long. To show the extinction of the dinosaurs, the timeline would have to be 6,500 meters, or 6.5 kilometers long. To show the rise of the Appalachian Mountains, the timeline would need to be 45 km long, and to show the formation of the Earth, the timeline would extend 450 kilometers, or about 280 miles!]

3. Niagara Falls, in addition to its wonder as a waterfall and fame as a honeymoon resort, also occupied an important historical location during the days of the Underground Railroad and the struggle against slavery. The swaying bridge across the falls required courage to cross—but it represented the final steps into Canada and freedom. Your students could research this aspect of the Falls as part of their U.S. History and Social Studies pursuits. The role played by rivers and streams along the entire route of the Underground Railway would make a fascinating research topic.

The Earth Today

The Earth
During the Ice Age
12,500 Years Ago

©1997 by the Regents of the University of California. LHS GEMS: *River Cutters*
May be duplicated for classroom or workshop use.

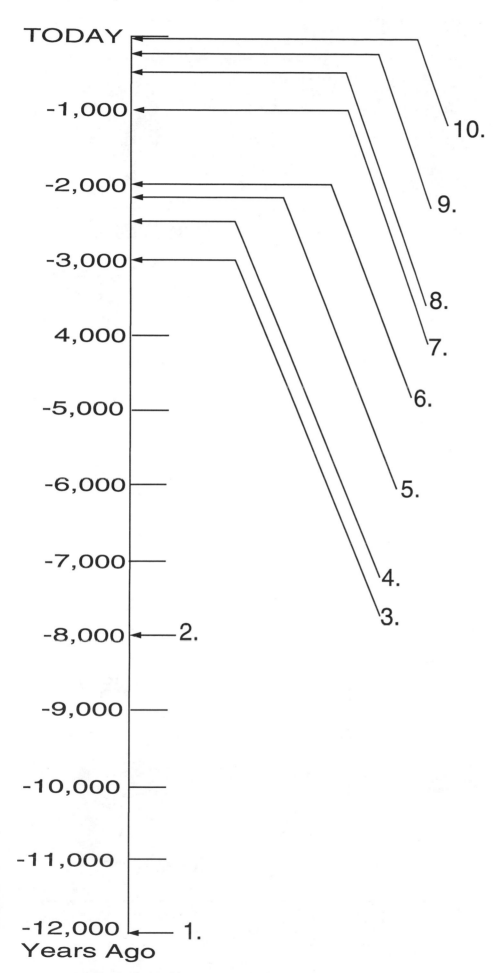

Timeline

©1997 by the Regents of the University of California. LHS GEMS: *River Cutters*
May be duplicated for classroom or workshop use.

Past Events

1. Land bridge migration takes place during ice ages, Last **Ice age ends** about 12,000 years ago. Mammoths and other large mammals begin to die off, possibly due to overhunting. **Increase drip rate to 5 drops/second.**

2. **Ice has melted** by about 8,000 years ago. After the end of the ice ages, the ice in North America has melted to present day levels. **Return drip rate to 2 drops/second.**

3. **Olmec** civilization flourishes in Mexico, approximately 3000 years ago. Unique stone monuments, statues, and designs have come down to us from Olmec culture.

4. **The Great Pyramid** was built in Egypt about 2,500 years ago, marking the zenith of a great ancient civilization.

5. **Great Wall of China**, about 2,200 years ago. The Emperor of the first united China ordered that a 4,000 mile long wall be built to protect against invaders.

6. **Roman Empire.** The Roman Empire was established in Europe, destined to have a powerful influence on the Western World.

7. **Ancient Ghana** was flourishing 1000 years ago in West Africa. Established hundreds of years before, this powerful kingdom was located to the north of the upper Niger River. (The modern nation of Ghana is farther south.)

Ancient Ghana

8. **Columbus sails** about 500 years ago, on his first voyage from Europe to the Americas. Native Americans have been there for thousands of years.

9. **United States established** about 225 years ago, with the signing of the Declaration of Independence.

10. **People land on the Moon** for the first time, about 30 years ago.

©1997 by the Regents of the University of California. LHS GEMS: *River Cutters*
May be duplicated for classroom or workshop use.

Past Events

1. Land bridge migration takes place during ice ages. Last **Ice age ends** about 12,000 years ago. Mammoths and other large mammals begin to die off, possibly due to overhunting. **Increase drip rate to 5 drops/second.**

2. **Ice has melted** by about 8,000 years ago. After the end of the ice ages, the ice in North America has melted to present day levels. **Return drip rate to 2 drops/second.**

3. **Olmec** civilization flourishes in Mexico, approximately 3000 years ago. Unique stone monuments and statues have come down to us from Olmec culture.

4. **The Great Pyramid** was built in Egypt about 2,500 years ago, marking the zenith of a great ancient civilization.

5. **Great Wall of China**, about 2,200 years ago. The Emperor of the first united China ordered that a 4,000 mile long wall be built to protect against invaders.

6. **Roman Empire.** The Roman Empire was established in Europe, destined to have a powerful influence on the Western World.

7. **Ancient Ghana** was flourishing 1,000 years ago in West Africa. Established hundreds of years before, this powerful African kingdom was located to the north of the upper Niger River. (The modern nation of Ghana is farther south.)

8. **Columbus sails** about 500 years ago, on his first voyage from Europe to the Americas. Native Americans have been there for thousands of years.

9. **United States declares its independence** about 225 years ago.

10. **People land on the Moon** for the first time, about 30 years ago.

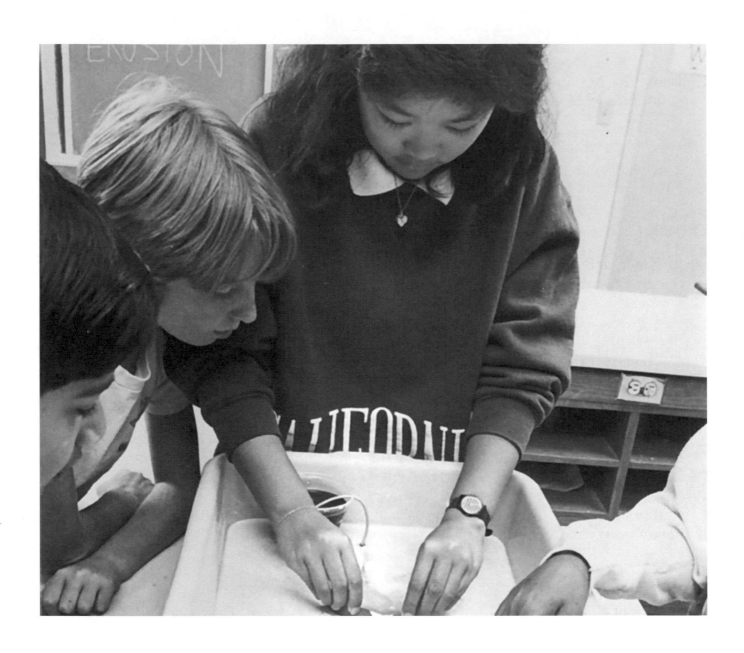

Session 4: Dams and Toxic Waste

Overview

In this session, your students combine the practical experience they gained in the first session with the geological information from the second session to observe their rivers in a more organized way. The teams conduct a five-minute river run and position flags as river features are identified. They will discover that as the river evolves, some features disappear and others emerge.

Through the placement of the river features flags, students are encouraged to determine the sequence of events in their rivers and to use appropriate terminology as they draw and label their model rivers. When the rivers are stopped, students build model dams and place simulated toxic waste dumps along the watershed.

Students then re-start the rivers to explore the impact of these human activities. As they place and test tiny dams and simulated toxic waste, they gain insight into the engineering principles, environmental considerations, and social factors that go into a complex decision-making process involving modern technology. They witness the consequences of dam failures and pollution through the impact on the river downstream.

This session provides an important opportunity for your students to develop their skills in systematically observing and recording the events in their river models. These skills are necessary for the controlled experiments that they will perform in Session 5, and the open-ended experiments that they are expected to design and conduct in the last session.

There is a lot packed into this session, so you may want to schedule it at a time when it's possible to extend the period by 15 or 20 minutes. Or, you can break it into two sessions. (See note on the top of this page.) During the session it is important to keep circulating to the various groups, making sure that the diatomaceous earth, the river model, and the drip rate are all as described in Session 1, and all students are participating in the process of recording events, creating toxic waste dumps and constructing dams, as well as drawing and labeling their developing rivers. Your conversations with the groups can reveal misconceptions students may have about the subject matter, as well as about experimentation and the use of models in general. Also, you'll have a chance to the degree to which they are applying the new ideas and vocabulary.

We've combined the study of toxic waste dumps and dams in this session to shorten the overall length of the unit. However, both of these topics are so important and complex that some teachers prefer to separate these topics into two separate lab sessions, followed by corresponding discussion sessions. While it would take more time, this approach would enable students to go into greater depth exploring what happens if they locate a dam in a different spot, measuring how long it takes toxic wastes to spread, and discussing relevant newspaper articles or television reports. If possible in your situation, we recommend separating the two activities.

*One teacher wrote to us that the toxic waste activities "are a great way to hook the students into an active interest in environmental issues—it is important that students are treated as scientists, giving them the sense of authority and foundation essential in pursuing the field. These models help provide a tangible link that is all too absent in schools—that **doing is knowing** link."*

What You Need

For the class:

- ❑ overhead projector, transparencies, and pens, or chalkboard and chalk
- ❑ 2 pitchers of blue-colored water
- ❑ 1 bottle of blue food coloring
- ❑ 1 bottle of red food coloring
- ❑ paper towels
- ❑ 1 bucket
- ❑ clock with a second hand
- ❑ *(optional)* 1 bottle of yellow food coloring
- ❑ *(optional)* 4–6 cotton swabs (such as Q-tips) dyed yellow at one end

See "Getting Ready," Step #3, for more on using the yellow food coloring.

For each team of 4–6 students:

- ❑ 1 river-cutting tub set-up (as used in Session 1)
- ❑ 1 sponge
- ❑ 1 piece of wood, 2" x 4" x 8"
- ❑ 1 aluminum pie pan
- ❑ 1 trowel or sturdy spoon
- ❑ river feature flags made in Session 2
- ❑ 2–3 3" x 5" strips of acetate or clear plastic film
- ❑ 2 clear plastic straws
- ❑ 4–6 cotton swabs (such as Q-tips) dyed red at one end
- ❑ scissors

For each student:

- ❑ 2 or more pieces of white paper
- ❑ 1 copy of both pages of the Geological Features handout (from Session 2)
- ❑ pencil

Getting Ready

Before the Day of the Activity

1. Cut 12–18 3" x 5" strips of acetate or clear plastic film to simulate tiny dams.

2. Soak 4–6 of the cotton swabs in red food coloring and allow them to dry out overnight. You can assist the drying process by placing them in an oven or microwave for a few minutes. Set these aside for use by student teams to represent toxic waste dumps.

3. Some teachers like to soak one swab for each tub in yellow food coloring, and to "plant" one of these in each of the tubs before class. Break the cotton swab in half so it can be hidden in the earth. Most teams will discover this "odd and forgotten" toxic waste emerge during the lesson.

4. The set up of materials is the same as in Session 1, with the addition of the river feature flags, white paper for recording observations, dams and simulated toxic waste.

The Day of the Activity

1. Replenish the supply of blue water in the dripper systems.

2. Set up the river-cutting tubs and dripper systems as before. Be sure to have the students re-slope their tubs.

3. If possible, arrange a large group discussion area away from the river systems. This will enable you to introduce the activity involving toxic waste dumps and dams, without the distraction of the model rivers being close at hand.

Setting the Scene—A Million Years Ago

1. Tell students that today they will observe rivers more systematically and see how *natural* changes in rivers compare to changes made by *people*. Explain that their tilted tubs represent a real continent sloping toward the seashore. The slope was caused when mountains were pushed upward many millions of years ago. Over the last two million years, this area was covered with ice more than one-mile thick, called a *glacier*. The glacier thawed and refroze about every 100,000 years, each time creating new lakes and rivers. Now, it is the end of the last Ice Age. The water in the dripper represents the melting of the last glacier. Let's see what happens as the ice melts!

2. Explain that in this session they will be cutting a five-minute river and documenting the features that evolve. The five-minute period represents 5,000 years, as the glacier slowly melts, and many rainstorms occur. After recording their observations, they will return to the present time and re-start their rivers to investigate the effects of modern technology—simulated dams and toxic waste dumps.

3. Have each team select a timekeeper. A second student should be appointed to the job of water watcher to make sure that the dripper system has an adequate water level. A third student should make and place river feature flags as needed, and a fourth should list the features in the order that they occur, on a blank sheet of paper. All students should watch the river system as it develops.

There is nothing "set in stone" about the five-minute river run period. Depending upon the investigative interest and discovery spirit of the students, you could, for example, increase this to ten minutes. However it is important to be consistent—to enable fair comparisons between rivers, all teams should run their rivers for the same amount of time. In general, let your teaching objectives and student interest determine the time spent running rivers. The longer a river runs, the more interesting the formations become—so long as students are learning, and you have the time, let students "cut deeper" into these activities.

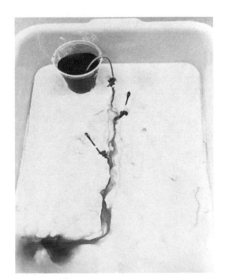

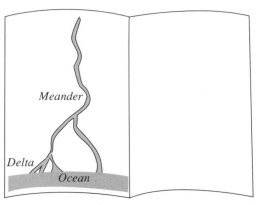

Sample student record after 5 minutes

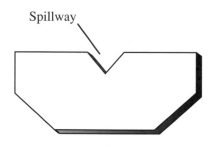

Spillway

Of course, an acetate strip is only a rough approximation of a dam. Some teachers and students may want to experiment with other materials or make more elaborate models, in order to obtain more realistic results.

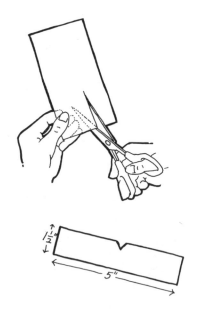

4. Tell the class that each team's timer should start timing a five-minute river as soon as the flow begins. As features occur, students should place an appropriately labeled flag to the left or right of the feature (so it does not interfere with the river flow).

5. Explain that after five minutes, the timekeeper should call time and the flow should be stopped. Students will then draw a map of the river system, noting the locations of river features.

6. Demonstrate, on the chalkboard or overhead projector, what a drawing might look like. If the paper supply is limited, you could have the students fold the paper in half, and draw the river after each five-minute period on one half. Most students will find it easier to use a full sheet of paper for each drawing.

7. Remind your students not to put their hands in the earth, or in any other way interfere with the river-cutting process. Flags should be set well to the side of the river, so they do not interfere if the river starts to meander or change course.

Cutting the River

1. Pass out river features flags, white paper, and pencils. Invite students to step back in time to when the last Ice Age ended—12,000 years ago. Have them start running their rivers. Circulate around the room to make sure that all is proceeding according to instructions and that the teams are working well together.

2. Encourage and assist the students as needed in planting the flags at appropriate times and places.

3. After the five minutes are up, make sure all the river flows have been turned off. Circulate to encourage students to draw maps of the river model and to label the features that they observe. Caution them to leave the river intact as they soon will re-start the dripper system for additional tests.

Setting the Scene for Human Interventions

1. If possible, have the teams come to a discussion area in the room, away from their model rivers. Re-focus the students' attention and explain that they will now play the role of engineers and geologists with the following two tasks:

    a. to construct a dam in a river in order to both control flooding and create a recreational reservoir; and

    b. to determine what happens if toxic waste dumps are placed too close to a river.

2. Show students the acetate strips that will serve as dams and demonstrate how to cut a notch in the acetate to simulate a spillway for the dam. Suggest they hollow out a reservoir uphill from where they plan to place the dam. Explain that real dams must be constructed where there are natural valleys, since scooping out huge amounts of Earth is too expensive.

3. Display the red-dyed cotton swabs that will simulate the toxic waste dumps. Demonstrate how to make a hole in the earth with a pencil, insert the swab dyed end down, and tamp down the earth around the stick. The unstained end of the swab serves as a marker for the toxic waste dump site.

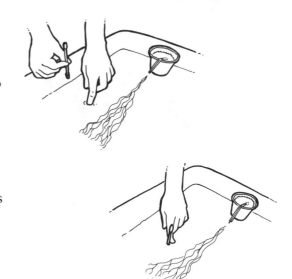

4. Let the teams discuss three or four locations. Suggest they position at least two of the toxic waste dumps close to the river. Although waste dumps are not supposed to be placed in such locations today, earlier in the century many companies did dump toxic wastes close to rivers.

5. Explain that movement of toxic waste through the soil can be monitored by drilling test plugs with a clear plastic straw. Demonstrate how to cut each of the two clear straws into four equal simulated "drills" (two for each student). If toxic waste is present, food coloring will appear in the plug of the clear straw. The pollution site can be marked with a flag.

Observing Effects of Dams and Dumps

1. Have the teams construct their dam and place several toxic dumps. Circulate to all teams, to see how they are doing.

2. When dam and dumps are placed, teams can re-start rivers for five more minutes. Explain that now the five-minute run stands for only 50 years—the time period in which dams and toxic waste have actually changed many river systems.

3. Circulate among the teams, asking questions to help focus student observations about **dams**: "Does a lake form?" "Are there problems with erosion?" "Is sediment being deposited behind the dam?" "How might the dam be changed?"

4. Ask questions about the **toxic waste dumps**: "Do you see any evidence that toxic waste has contaminated the river?" "Where is the toxic waste underground?" (Use the clear plastic "drill.") You can also ask questions to assess their understanding of models in science, such as "What did this model help you find out," "Why did we need to use a model in this case?" "How can models be misleading?"

5. When the five minutes are up, ask all students to stop the drippers and record their rivers on another sheet (or half-sheet) of paper. Have them draw locations of dams and toxic waste dumps, label geologic features, and show the channels of the river. Tell the students to show the results of their "drilling" to determine what happened to the toxic waste.

6. Have students finish drawing and clean up. If not needed by the next class, keep river systems intact for the next time. As the tubs sit, the movement of the toxic waste will become even more apparent with time.

An excellent journal extension is to ask the students to tell the story of this investigation as though they were investigating the effects of human intervention in a real river system. They could use their drawings of the labeled river systems to illustrate their stories.

A mathematics extension is to have students figure out the scale of the model, given the assumption that the real river is, for example, 100 meters at the widest point in the channel. Another extension is for students to measure the rate at which toxic waste spreads through the ground water.

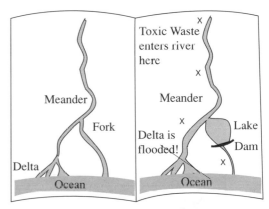

Sample student record after second 5-minute run

24 Bars for a River Mural

by Robert Hass

—for Mark Baldridge and Shane Bagleton

Long one, always a flowing, always in place, teach us silence
     and surprise

       ·

     —watery mind

       ·

It is good sometimes to stand silent by a river

       ·

Kingfishers flash in the bright shallows
     Swallows veering in the insect dusk

       ·

As if each life were a long thought flowing

       ·

Now and then now and then now

       ·

What you are feeling is a river

       ·

Trout leap, heron fish in the purling eddies

       ·

Roars down canyons, carves channels

       ·

Boils over rocks in a white foaming

       ·

The grain of wood is a river

       ·

The thrum of blood in the blue vein is a river

       ·

She fought the current

       ·

He gave himself to the river's will

       ·

Alder leaves, oak, willow,
     loosed from the muddy banks

       ·

Somebody's roof, chicken coop, pet hog, bridal dress
     gone downriver, gone, in the great cleansing

       ·

Blackbird sittin on the tree of life, they sang,
     he hears the Jordan roll

       ·

Cross that river to Freedom Land, they sang

       ·

Old names: Susquehanna, Shenandoah, Mississippi

       ·

Fish are jumping, they sang, and the cotton is high

       ·

Cloud-towers, cloud-mirrors in the reedy channels

       ·

Uprivering gulls, sand bars, silted islands

       ·

This is an end, this is something else

       ·

Salt grass, salt smell, and the sea

Session 5: Discussing the Results of River Models

Overview

In this session, your students discuss the results of the previous session, and consider how they may apply to real rivers today. This naturally leads to more wide-ranging discussions concerning the environmental impacts of technology and human interference on river systems. Students are encouraged to discuss the benefits and drawbacks of such interference, and what might be done to increase the benefits while reducing detrimental impacts on the environment.

What You Need

For the class:
- ❑ overhead projector, transparencies, and pens, or chalkboard and chalk

For each student:
- ❑ collection of earth photographs and geology textbooks with photos of river features and geological landscapes
- ❑ 1–2 pieces of lined paper
- ❑ 1 pencil

Getting Ready

If they are available, have the river-cutting tubs from the previous session lined up so that students may check them at the beginning of the class.

Discussing the Results

1. As students enter the classroom, ask them to quickly check their river systems from the previous session, then get out their drawings and lists of river features.

2. Explain that the purpose of this session is to discuss how rivers change *naturally* over time as compared to *changes made by people*. To do this they will compare the results of the first five-minute run in the last session with the second five-minute run. Ask, "How do the results of these runs differ?" "What does this tell us about the ways natural processes differ from changes made by people?"

3. Invite students to add to the class list of river features that was started in the second session. As you record their observations, ask if the feature appeared in the early stages of the river or in its later development.

photo by G. Donald Bain, University of California at Berkeley

This photograph shows Shasta Dam in California, with Shasta Lake which was formed when the dam was built. The peak in the far distance is Mount Shasta. The large building in the foreground is an electrical generating station, powered by water which flows through large pipes from the bottom of the dam. Shasta Dam provides electrical power, flood control, and a recreational lake. If there is a dam in your state or region, try to get a photo of it, find out why it was built and what functions it serves today.

4. Next, have each team report the results of their investigations of dams, and encourage them to discuss how dams work, how silt builds, how they leak, or whatever else they observed regarding dams. Some possible topics to discuss are:

- What are the benefits of dams? [flood control, irrigation, generation of electrical power, lakes, and recreation]

- What are some drawbacks of dams? [Large areas of open fields or wilderness areas are flooded. Downriver systems are disrupted. The free passage of fish is impeded. The enrichment of soil by periodic flooding is reduced.]

- What problems might engineers who build and maintain dams encounter? [Dams must be strong enough and high enough to resist occasional serious flooding. Also, eventually, silt builds up behind the dam and makes it ineffective.]

- Can you think of ways to deal with these problems? [Modern dams are built stronger than they used to be, but unusual flooding can still overwhelm dams. Silt is a very difficult problem to deal with, and many dams simply have to be abandoned as sites for electrical power generation when they silt up.]

- Are there any dams in our local area? What are the benefits or problems associated with these dams?

5. Conduct a similar discussion concerning the toxic waste dump sites. Consider the environmental impact with questions like these: "How far did the toxic waste travel?" "What does this mean when considering wells and city water supplies?" "Where are the best places to bury toxic wastes?" "Should they be buried at all?"

6. Ask students, "What are other ways that human activities affect natural river systems?" [Encourage all responses. Students may bring up increased erosion due to clearing of land, so valuable topsoil is lost. Another problem is building on the floodplain of rivers, so that when periodic flooding occurs people lose their homes and livelihoods.]

7. Focus students' attention on the time scales represented by their models. "How much time was represented in the first five-minute period, when there were no human interventions?" [The changes in river systems occurred over thousands and even millions of years.] "How much time was needed to change the river systems by human intervention?" [Significant changes could occur in only a few years.]

8. Point out that dams and toxic waste dumps are just two ways humans have changed the environment. Although a change may seem safe and reasonable at the time, in future years problems may arise. Ask "What are some other examples of how changes in the environment, or new technologies, can have unanticipated side effects?" [possible examples include: pollution-related problems, such as acid rain; clearing of hillsides for timber or to create pastureland has increased erosion in some areas; extinguishing forest fires changes tree diversity, since "natural" forest fires, started by lightning, are not allowed to burn; construction of roads and cities makes it impossible for certain species to maintain their home ranges or migrate to other areas. There are many other examples.]

9. Encourage student discussion. If students raise further issues related to dam construction or toxic waste, mention that they will have the opportunity to design their own investigations with the river models later in the unit. You may also want to assign a brief essay on what they learned from their investigation of dams and/or toxic waste.

10. Ask students, "What did the model help you do in this activity?" [Find out more about how river systems can be affected by human intervention such as dams and toxic waste] Ask, "Does the model *alone* provide enough evidence to make decisions about possible human interventions? [No!] "What other types of data should scientists gather to make decisions about toxic waste dumps?" [actual cores drilled on site] "To make decisions about dams?" [measurements of sediment behind dams and actual results of flooding]

11. Conclude by asking students for their opinions on why the time for the runs was kept the same—five minutes—for all teams. [If students do not mention it, explain that keeping the time the same makes it possible to compare all rivers fairly. The idea of a fair test will be explained in more detail in the next session.

If you planted swabs with yellow food coloring to simulate secret or previously unknown toxic waste dumps, and your students discovered this, you will want to discus how this models the fact that unexpected toxic waste dumps and other pollution can and do crop up unexpectedly. Such toxic waste could derive, for example, from waste that has been illegally dumped or that was dumped before reporting was required.

Session 6: River Experiments—Age or Slope?
Overview

In previous sessions your students used models to gain insight into the natural processes that shape landforms, and the ways that human activities can impact river systems. The laboratory method was to systematically observe and record what happened in their models. That was a fairly simple use of a model since students gradually developed new ideas and insights during the running of a single model river. **In this session, your students will perform controlled experiments to test alternative theories about how different kinds of river valleys are formed.** This is a more sophisticated use of models because your students must first clarify their theories, then conduct two simultaneous river runs to compare the effects of different variables.

The students will begin by looking at photographs of the Green River Valley and the Sacramento River Valley. They will compare the two river valleys, and discuss their own theories for why one is so steep and the other so broad and shallow. They will then use their river models to conduct a controlled experiment to compare these two alternative theories: that the difference between these two rivers is due to the age of the river versus the idea that it is caused by differences in the slope of the terrain. At the end of the period, the students discuss their results, then learn about additional evidence to help them further consider the affects of age and slope on river development.

Within the limitations of the models in these experiments, your students are likely to find that the most dramatic differences between rivers occur as a result of differences in slope. However, if you can find a much larger stream table (3' to 4' long) and can run the river for a longer period of time (say, 2 hours) the model will be much more effective in illustrating how increasing age of a river also changes the features.

It's helpful to keep in mind that, initially, many students think of experimentation as a method of trying things out or producing a desired outcome, but with instruction they can learn how scientists use experiments to test their theories. In addition, students sometimes have difficulty interpreting the results of experiments and tend to look just for evidence that supports their prior beliefs. It is also important to recognize that in science there are no perfect models and no perfectly controlled experiments. Yet using models and conducting controlled experiments are still very useful techniques for gaining insight into natural processes. The best that a scientist can do is to continuously improve the model and do a better job of controlling all of the important variables.

What You Need

For the class:
- ❑ 2 pitchers of blue-colored water
- ❑ 1 bottle of blue food coloring
- ❑ paper towels
- ❑ 1 bucket

For each team of 4–6 students:
- ❑ 1 river-cutting tub set-up as used in Session 1
- ❑ 1 sponge
- ❑ 1 piece of wood, 2" x 4" x 8"
- ❑ 1 aluminum pie pan
- ❑ 1 trowel or sturdy spoon
- ❑ river feature flags

For each student:
- ❑ 1 copy of the Two River Valleys handout (master on page 65)
- ❑ 2 or more pieces of white paper
- ❑ pencil

You will probably want to remove the cotton swabs. However, don't be concerned about the discoloration caused by the red and/or yellow coloring. It tends to diffuse (a lesson in itself). In addition, this slight coloration can sometimes enhance the visual appearance of river features.

Getting Ready

1. Replenish the supply of blue water in the dripper system.

2. Set up the river model as in the previous sessions. Have students re-slope tubs before cutting rivers. Students will need a piece of wood to adjust the slope of the tubs when they do the activity.

What Are Your Students' Ideas?

1. Acknowledge that students have probably already developed theories about how water shapes the land. The purpose of this session is to find out what some of their theories are and to experiment with models to test different theories.

2. Pass out the Two River Valleys handout, asking students to discuss differences between the shapes of the two *river valleys*—the basins the rivers flow through—as shown in the photographs. Make certain that all students realize that the Green River Valley is very steep and narrow compared to its depth, while the Sacramento River Valley is shallow and very wide. Students might also notice that the Green River is in a mountainous area. It is even possible to see layers of sedimentary rock that the river has eroded. The Sacramento River lies in a broad, flat floodplain, where many farms are now located.

Why are some river valleys broad and shallow...

3. Ask the students to write a few sentences at the bottom of the handout, explaining what they think may have **caused** the shapes of these river valleys to be so different.

4. Collect the students' papers and save them to compare with their ideas after completing the activity—as a pre-post assessment task.

5. Invite the students to briefly explain their different theories. Paraphrase their ideas and list them on the chalkboard or butcher paper, but avoid extended discussion at this point. If they do not bring up the following two theories, be sure to mention them and add them to the list.

- The Green River flows through steeply sloped mountainous terrain, while the Sacramento River flows through flat terrain, with a very shallow slope. A steeper slope would cause the river to cut more deeply into the underlying rock and soil.

- Maybe one river is much older than the other. Perhaps the Green River is older and has cut much more deeply into the ground; or maybe the Sacramento River is older, and has had time to erode the entire region so it is flat.

Many of the farms along the Sacramento River were flooded in January, 1997, when heavy rains combined with warm weather that melted snow in the mountains at the source of the Sacramento River and its tributaries.

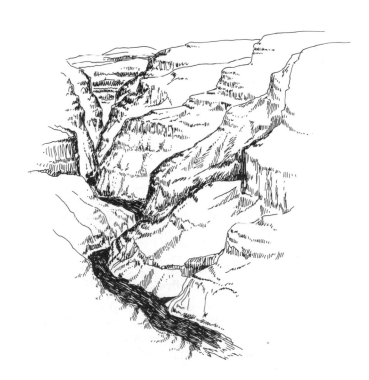

...while other river valleys are narrow and deep?

All of the investigations using
models involve systematic
observations. In controlled
experiments, two models are
observed and compared. In
order to draw a valid
conclusion from the
experiment, the two models
must differ in only one way.

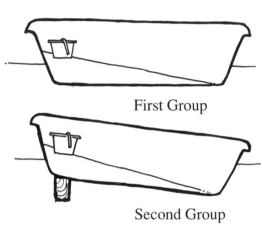

First Group

Second Group

Conducting Controlled Experiments

What Is the Effect of Slope?

1. Ask students how they might use their river models to
determine which of two factors—slope or age—is the most
likely explanation for the difference between the Green and
Sacramento River Valleys. If students do not suggest it,
explain that a scientific approach to the question would be to
conduct a **controlled experiment**, which is a "fair test," that in
this case can be used to compare two different possible
explanations.

2. Tell the students that you would like two groups to work
together, with their river models side-by-side. First, all
groups will test the idea that slope makes a difference. The
two groups should first see if they agree on how they expect
slope to affect the river. Then, they should level their
diatomaceous earth, using the block of wood to make the
slopes exactly the same. One group should place its tub flat
on the table, while the other group uses the block of wood to
increase the steepness of the slope.

3. Explain that in order for the experiment to be a fair test of
whether or not slope makes a difference, everything else must
be the same. Ask, "If, for example one group has a faster drip
rate, and its river is deeper than the other, can we be sure
that's due to slope?" [No, the deeper river could be due to the
faster drip rate!]

4. Point out that to find out if slope really makes a difference,
it is very important that the drip rates, the flatness of the
terrain, and all other **variables** (things that also might make a
difference) are exactly the same. Only the slope (the test
variable) should be different.

5. Tell the groups to run their rivers for five minutes,
beginning and ending at the same time. Ask them to imagine
that a five-minute run equals 5,000 years of erosion from
repeated rainstorms.

6. While the rivers are running, circulate asking focusing
questions, such as: "What differences do you see so far?" "Is
that what you expected?"

7. After the rivers have run for five minutes, the two groups
will compare the two rivers. They should place flags marking
river features. Each student should draw both rivers on a
blank sheet of paper, using words and labels to explain how
they are different. Have the students get started. Tell them
that they should not disturb the rivers after drawing them.

8. When students have finished drawing the two rivers, ask teams to describe differences. Most groups will probably notice that the more steeply sloped terrain now has a river valley that looks more like the Green River in that it cuts more deeply. However, both river valleys will probably be somewhat straight at this point, with few meanders.

What Is the Effect of Age?

1. Tell students they will now see what happens as the rivers age. They should predict how they think the rivers will change if they run the rivers another ten minutes—representing an additional 10,000 years of natural erosion and deposition. They should then re-start their rivers. As the rivers run, they should notice how river features change, using flags to remember where the features were located in the younger rivers.

2. During this run, circulate, asking questions to focus comparison of younger and older rivers: "Have you seen any changes yet?" "Does the period of time seem to make as much difference as the slope?"

3. When the teams have finished a ten minute run, have each student again draw both rivers, noting how their features have changed. Tell the students to lay their drawings next to each other so they can compare old and young rivers with the same slope, and so they can also compare rivers of the same age with different slope. Ask the combined teams to discuss:

• What is the effect of age? [Older rivers will probably show more meanders and larger deltas, and will be cut more deeply. Some may have developed oxbow lakes or other features that did not show up on the younger rivers.]

• What is the effect of slope for an old river? [The old shallow river will probably look a little more like the Sacramento River, with meanders. The old steep river will probably look more like the Green River now, with more meanders and also cutting more deeply into the surface. However, the difference between the younger and older river may not be pronounced. A longer stream table and longer period of time are usually needed to bring out the differences.]

4. After a few minutes, call the class together and ask groups to report on their findings.

5. Ask the students which theory they think is better supported by their experiments. [The results may differ, but in general, slope tends to make the more evident difference. Accept your students' ideas, emphasizing that their conclusions should flow from what they actually observed.] Invite students to wander around the room for a few minutes, so they can see the results of the other groups.

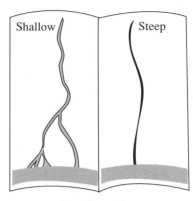

Sample student drawings of young rivers

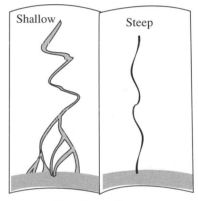

Sample student drawings of old rivers

6. Ask students what they think might happen if they let their rivers run for 2–3 **hours**, removing water from the "sea," and adding water to the dripper as needed. Could the river valley ever get deeper than sea level? [No.] How would the river change? [Valleys would probably get wider, meanders more extreme] How might the 2–3 hour model be a better model of the way rivers change in the real world? [Real rivers are thousands of years old, so the model would be closer to the real thing.]

Conclusion

1. Tell students that no model or experiment can be perfect. Models can always be improved to make them more realistic, and experiments can be improved to control more of the variables. Ask if they can think of any improvements in the river models or the experiments. Add any ideas mentioned to a class list of possible experiments for the next session.

2. Remind the students that their experiments have been with models, not real rivers. Although models are useful—because it is not possible to go back in time to see how the Green and Sacramento Rivers really formed— they provide only one kind of evidence. Ask the students if they can think of any other kinds of evidence they might look for to determine why the river valleys are so different.

3. Inform students that scientists have analyzed the material in the deltas of both rivers. They found that the Sacramento River delta is made of very fine silt while the Green River delta has layers of silt, but also layers of sand and even large pebbles. What does this additional evidence tell us about why these river valleys are so different? [It supports the idea that slope was the most important factor, since a steeper slope means a faster river that could carry heavier sediments.]

4. You may want to add that the portion of the Sacramento River in the photo is only a little above sea level. The Green River, however, runs through terrain that is nearly a mile above sea level. It is part of the Colorado Plateau that has been pushed upwards to its present height over the last ten million years. The river cut deeper and deeper as the land rose higher and higher. So, the vast differences in the appearance of the Green and Sacramento Rivers is mainly due to the slope of the land.

5. Ask students to describe their local landscape. Which direction do rivers or creeks run? What does that say about the slope of the land? Are there any river valleys in your area? Are they more like the Sacramento or the Green—why?

6. Conclude by asking students to explain why using models to conduct controlled experiments is especially helpful in finding out how water shapes the land. [Controlled experiments make it possible to compare and test different theories.]

Student suggestions for improvement will help you assess their understanding of controlled experimentation and the effective use of models.

To see if your students can transfer their new understanding to different river valleys, show them pictures of the Grand Canyon (Colorado River) and the Mississippi. Ask them why they think these river valleys are so different, and how they might find out if their explanations are valid.

TWO RIVER VALLEYS

This is the Green River Valley in Colorado. It cuts deeply into the layers of rock and soil. The bank of the river is several hundred feet high.

This is the Sacramento River Valley in California. The banks of the river are just a few feet high. Frequent floods have made the surrounding farmland very fertile.

photos by Lisa Wells, Vanderbilt University

1. Compare these two meandering rivers. In your opinion, what might explain why one river has cut so deeply into the rock and soil, while the other river has cut a very shallow basin?

2. What evidence—from what you can see in the pictures, or from any experiments you may have done—supports your theory?

© 1997 by The Regents of the University of California. LHS GEMS: *River Cutters*.
May be duplicated for classroom or workshop use.

MEANDEASMEANDERS

Session 7: Designing Your Own Experiments

Overview

This is the culminating activity in the *River Cutters* unit. Up to this point, your students have explored the materials and investigated questions that you defined for them, and used methods that you prescribed. Now it's time for them to take off in their own directions.

An inquiry designed and carried out by students is referred to as a "full investigation" in the *National Science Education Standards*. According to the *Standards*, students should have an opportunity to conduct a full investigation at least once a year. *River Cutters* provides an excellent opportunity for your students do this. It's a great way to end the unit, since they will be very interested in—and tend to remember—a project that they selected. It also serves an open-ended authentic assessment, in which students apply what they have learned so far in the unit to questions *they* feel are important.

It is recommended that you divide this session into three class periods. One period for your students to plan their experiments; one for them to conduct the experiments; and a third period for each team to present their results. Allow a day or two between the first and second class periods so you and they will have time to gather any special materials they might need.

What You Need

For the class:
- ❐ 2 pitchers of blue-colored water
- ❐ 1 bottle of blue food coloring
- ❐ paper towels
- ❐ 1 bucket
- ❐ 1 chalkboard and chalk or butcher paper and marker

For each team of 4–6 students:
- ❐ 1 copy of "Sample Research Questions" sheet (page 70)
- ❐ 1 river cutter tub set-up
- ❐ 1 sponge
- ❐ 1 piece of wood, 2" x 4" x 8"
- ❐ 1 aluminum pie pan
- ❐ 1 trowel or sturdy spoon
- ❐ special materials requested by student teams

For each student:
- ❐ several sheets of paper
- ❐ pencils

Getting Ready

Plan the schedule so there are at least a couple of days between the planning session and the experimenting session, so you'll have time to gather any special materials that might be needed. The third period should be shortly after the students finish their experiments, while their results are still fresh in their minds.

Students Plan Their Own Experiments (Period 1)

Allowing time for your students to plan their experiments is a very important aspect of this last session. Planning time is needed for your students to move from a vague idea to a well-framed question and an experimental procedure that they feel enthusiastic about carrying out.

1. Invite your students to work in their groups to design and conduct their own investigations using their experimental river models.

2. Hand out the "Sample Research Questions" sheet to each team and discuss these possible experiments. For each one, ask the students: "What is the question that the investigation is designed to answer or find out more about?" "What kind of investigation is planned—is it a systematic observation and recording? or a controlled experiment?" [The first two examples are controlled experiments; the next two are systematic observations. **There are many other modes of scientific investigation, not just these two kinds.**]

3. If the investigation being discussed is a controlled experiment, also ask, "What is the test variable?" [with or without a levee; with or without plants] Also ask, "Is this a fair test?" "if not, how can the experiment be improved?" [students should look for uncontrolled variables]

4. Tell the class that by the end of the period you would like them to provide you with a one-page summary which describes:

   a. The question they intend to investigate.

   b. A plan for how they will use river models to address the question.

   c. A list of special materials, besides their river models, that they will need.

5. Before they break up into groups, have the class brainstorm some possible questions to research. List these on the chalkboard or on butcher paper.

6. Urge students to apply what they have learned in the unit in planning their experiments. They should consider: how flowing water shapes the land by erosion and deposition; the role of slope, terrain, and time in the creation of landforms; an effort to control variables; and the time scale represented by their experiments.

7. Tell the students that they may need to rephrase their question in a way that makes it more possible to address with a systematic observation or an experiment that uses the river models.

8. Give the groups a few minutes to start planning on their own, then circulate among them offering suggestions as needed. Student groups will vary in their abilities to design controlled experiments and/or model-related investigations. It is more important to encourage them to pursue their interests and take charge of their investigations than to come up with the very best experimental plan.

9. At the end of class, collect a paper from each team, describing their proposed experiment/investigation. Read these over to determine what materials will be needed for the next class period, and to think about any suggestions you might make to improve the experiments.

10. As noted above, the next page includes some suggestions, based on our experience with this unit over many years, to assist you and your students in discussing investigations. We've also included a few more suggestions in the box below, to help spur more ideas. You and your students will probably come up with many of your own. The GEMS program would love to hear about them!

RESEARCH QUESTION: Do waterfalls travel upstream or downstream? One group of students thought that waterfalls did travel, but were not sure in which direction. They built up a hill in the tub, with a "cliff" of diatomaceous earth. They ran a river. One student marked the position of the waterfall with toothpicks while another students called "time" every minute, and the others drew and took notes.

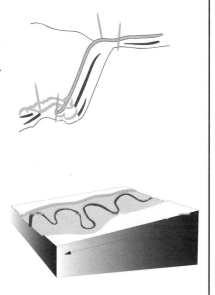

RESEARCH QUESTION: What geological features are found in areas with frequent droughts and floods? In certain areas of the country it is common for there to be very little rain for many years in a row (drought), and then a year when there is more rain than normal (flood). Students can simulate these conditions by adjusting the drip rate—five minutes at two drips/second, followed by one minute at six drips/second, and so on. They can compare the features they observe—such as floodplains and braided channels—with geological features in areas where these drought/flood conditions are common.

SAMPLE RESEARCH QUESTIONS

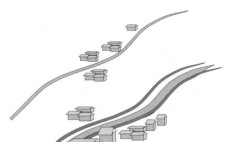

RESEARCH QUESTION: What happens if you build levees to control floods?

Having read about what happened during a large flood, a team of students decided to see if they could protect a city by building walls, or levees, on both sides of a river. They ran two rivers for five minutes, representing 5000 years. They then used extra diatomaceous earth to reinforce the banks of one of the rivers. They built a small city along the banks of both rivers, using houses from a Monopoly™ game. They then increased the rate of flow from the drippers and observed whether or not the towns were flooded, and how extensive the flooding was. They wanted to find out if the town with the levee "survived" with less flooding than the town without the levee.

RESEARCH QUESTION: How will plants affect erosion?

Some seeds will germinate and grow in diatomaceous earth. One group of students grew bean seeds in one part of a tub. (Grass and alfalfa seeds will also sprout in diatomaceous earth.) When the plants took root, they tilted the tub, and used a watering can equally on all of the surfaces. They watched to see if the area with the plants eroded more slowly than the area without the plants .

RESEARCH QUESTION: How do river meanders change over time?

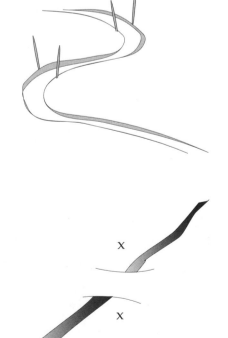

One group of students wondered whether meanders grew toward the outside or the inside of the curve. They also wanted to know if meanders traveled upstream or downstream over time. They decided to answer this question by observing and recording a river over a 20-minute period, to represent 20,000 years. One student was the timer. Another placed toothpicks on the inside and outside bends of meanders, while the others drew and took notes on what happened every two minutes.

RESEARCH QUESTION: What happens to toxic wastes in the soil?

Water below the surface of the ground is called the water table. In a dry riverbed, water may still be flowing underground where it can still be "tapped into" by plant roots and wells. One group of students decided to investigate this. They placed "toxic wastes" at several locations in their river model and let it run for a long time. They probed the entire tub to see what happened to it. They also dug wells and watched to see if these filled with toxic wastes.

© 1997 by The Regents of the University of California. LHS GEMS: *River Cutters*.
May be duplicated for classroom or workshop use.

Conducting the Experiments (Period 2)

1. Provide one class period for the students to conduct their experiments/investigations. Circulate, providing assistance and asking questions, to maintain focus on the research question and how the experiment can help answer it.

2. After the experiments have been performed, ask each team (or each individual) to prepare a short lab report, describing their team's:

> a. **Research Question.** What question is your experiment designed to address?

> b. **Procedure.** Draw and label your experimental setup, and describe what you did. Explain the conditions and period of time the simulation is intended to represent. (If a controlled experiment, identify the test variable and explain how you attempted to control all other variables.)

> c. **Results**. Sketch and describe your results.

> d. **Conclusion.** Write a conclusion, explaining how your results answered (or did not answer) your research question.

> e. **Recommendations.** If your experiment has any practical applications, what are they?

Reporting the Results (Period 3)

1. Allow time for each group to report on its results to the rest of the class.

2. When each group finishes its report, invite other students to ask questions or comment. If the students do not have questions, you might ask the team how they refined their original question, how their experiment might apply to the local area, or what they would like to do, if they had more time, to improve the experiment.

3. Briefly summarize the conclusions and recommendations of each team on the chalkboard or butcher paper. When teams are finished, briefly list the findings of the class.

4. Tell your class that **scientists** from many different fields use models to test alternative theories. Although further evidence is almost always needed to confirm theories tested in this way, models are a very important way to gain insight into processes—like those that form river systems or build mountains—which take thousands or millions of years in the real world.

It is important to allow a full period for teams to report their results. Most students will have a lot to say about their experiments, and it is best if they are not rushed. The discussion that occurs after each presentation is probably the best way for your students to learn what it feels like to belong to a scientific community.

On the next page we reprint an article showing the use of a model related to rivers in the work of Hsieh Wen Shen, a professor of mechanical engineering at U.C. Berkeley and an expert on river dynamics. Models of many kinds (including computer simulations) are in constant use by scientists and mathematicians. A copy of the article is included at the back of the book in case you want to share it and the questions with your class.

See "Going Further" for ways to expand this unit and "Assessment Suggestions" for some ideas on ways to evaluate what your students have learned from this unit.

5. Mention that **engineers** also use models, in very practical ways, to see how something will work. For example, they might use models to see what will happen to a river with or without levees, when flooding occurs. While models will not show exactly what will happen, they can often help pinpoint problems that may occur, and perhaps prevent costly mistakes.

6. Ask: "How have you acted like scientists and/or engineers in this unit?" "What's something *you have done* to find out how water slopes the land?" "What's something *you have done* to pinpoint a problem or find a solution that might work?" "Can you think of ways you might use models or controlled experiments to help you learn more about a topic you're interested in?"

Shen's Model Helps Undo 'Improvements' to a River

The largest ecological restoration project ever attempted in the United States will be guided in part by a model of a river built by Hsieh Wen Shen, professor of mechanical engineering and an expert on river dynamics.

Shen demonstrated his 60- by 100-foot model recently for the South Florida Water Management District officials who are directing the Kissimmee River Restoration Project, a $150 -$200 million Florida program to return the channelized river to its natural state.

Shen's three-year study will help officials decide the fate of the river that carries water from Lake Kissimmee to Lake Okeechobee in South Florida.

The Army Corps of Engineers channelized the river in the '60s, after earlier hurricanes whetted sediment for flood control. By 1971, the formerly shallow, meandering 98-mile river was a 52-mile canal. But the ecological impact proved devastating. Some 40,000 acres of wetlands disappeared, driving away 90 percent of the water birds.

Shen points out that his calculations have to take into account water flow under all circumstances. A system that drains water too quickly after intense rains could pose a natural disaster. —Jesús Mena

Reprinted from *The Berkeleyan*, a newspaper for faculty and staff of the University of California at Berkeley.

QUESTIONS

1. What do you think the "restoration project" is intended to accomplish?

2. What kind of information do you think Dr. Shen's model provided?

3. Imagine that you are in charge of the South Florida Water Management District. What questions would you ask Dr. Shen about his model?

4. Would data from Dr. Shen's model by itself be enough for you to decide what to do? If not, what other types of data might you need?

Hsieh Wen Shen (photo by Susan Spann)

Going Further *(for the entire unit)*

1. Encourage your students to undertake a long-term project involving their river models. This could involve, for example, a day-to-day tracking of river features over a longer period of time with a much slower drip rate.

2. Have students create a model or a drawing of a river project that they design which includes a dam and reservoir. The reservoir should be able to be used both as a source of water and a recreation area by the community. Plans might also include picnic areas, bathrooms, vegetation and animal life, and a source of energy for lighting and other needs.

3. Take students on a hike in the rain to observe natural storm runoff and erosion.

4. Model rivers can be photographed at different intervals as an accurate record of changes over time. A regular camera or a video camera with a "time lapse" feature can be used. The river features can be highlighted for photography by placing a bright light at a low angle to the side of the tub. The resultant shadow effect emphasizes the river features.

5. A local issue on dam construction, water pollution, or toxic waste disposal can be examined. Representatives of industry and environmental groups could be invited to school to discuss these issues. After students have gathered information, they could hold a debate on the pros and cons of the issue.

6. Have students research cases of ground water pollution by toxic waste dumps. Famous cases include Love Canal, Times Beach, and Hanford, Washington.

7. The "Behind the Scenes" section contains information on how Robert E. Horton has applied mathematics to river tributary systems. Students could do further research on this topic.

8. Have students research recent floods, such as the Mississippi flood of 1996, and the California, Ohio/Kentucky, and North Dakota floods of early 1997. Information about the floods can be found in periodicals and on the Internet. One source is the U.S. Geological Survey site at http://www.usgs.gov/

9. Have students research the huge water release of March, 1996, from the Glen Canyon Dam into the Grand Canyon, including reading an article from the "Science Times" section of the Feb. 25, 1997 *New York Times*. This was done as a research project to see how a restoration of water flow would impact the ecosystems within the Canyon. It was the first time that the Grand Canyon was flooded in the 33 years since the dam was built. Water flow increased from 8,000 cubic feet per second (ft^3/sec) to 45,000 ft^3/sec.

10. Assign student teams to design a different dripper system. Teams can draw their ideas or use materials and build a working model. You might ask each team: Can the rate of the drip be adjusted? Does it act more like a rainstorm or melting snow? What kind of river do think it will create?

74

Behind the Scenes

One of the most remarkable maps of the United States ever produced is entitled "Land Forms and Drainage of the 48 States." Constructed with the aid of satellite imagery, this beautiful and accurately shaded black & white map clearly illustrates the western mountain ranges from the Rockies to the Sierras and the smaller ranges on the East Coast. In between is the huge drainage basin that feeds the Mississippi River. (See the box at the bottom of this page for how to obtain this map for your classroom.)

Wherever you may live in the contiguous 48 states, you can find your location on the map, and determine where local rainfall is likely to travel on its journey to the sea. Your efforts will be greatly aided by a magnifying glass, which will reveal the name of every major river. (Similar maps exist of Hawaii and Alaska.)

The most obvious feature of the map is the huge Mississippi River Basin, which is bounded by the Allegheny Mountains on the East and the Rocky Mountains on the West. The land is sloped gradually upwards from the Mississippi to these mountain ranges. That is why nearly all of the rivers in central North America empty into the Mississippi. The eastern mountain ranges are by far the oldest, being thrust upwards between about 450 million years ago and 350 million years ago. The Rocky Mountains are relatively "young." They were thrust upward from a flat plain about 70 million years ago, and in some areas the uplift continues even today.

During the last Ice Age, the polar ice cap extended as far south as the current location of New York City. When the huge glaciers began to melt they changed the course of rivers. The Missouri and Ohio Rivers, for example, which had formerly drained to the Atlantic, changed their courses so that they fed the Mississippi. The current courses of most rivers in the northern part of the country were established during this time, about 10 thousand years ago. The wide, meandering, and sometimes braided channels of rivers in the central parts of the country can be explained by the thousands of years that they have flowed across very gently sloping plains.

The deep river-cut canyons of the Southwest, including the Grand Canyon, have a different history. Starting about 10 million years ago, the Colorado Plateau was thrust upwards, as much as three miles high at one point. As the land rose, the rivers cut deeper and deeper into the landscape. Since the rocky sandstone terrain was more resistant to erosion than soil, the sides of the canyons remained relatively steep. The Colorado Plateau stopped rising about 5 million years ago, and today the highest parts are only a little more than a mile above sea level. Since the glaciers never reached as far south as Colorado, the rivers in this area have been slowly changing over the past ten million years.

Map Name: Landforms of the U.S.
USGS Map I-2206, published 1991
Map Authors: Gail Thelin and Richard Pike
Order from: United States Geological Service (USGS)—Denver
1-800-435-7627
fax: (303) 202-4693
$ 4.00 per copy plus $ 3.50 handling, per order

Diatomaceous Earth

The name of this substance derives from small organisms named diatoms. **Diatoms** are microscopic algae eaten by many marine animals. The cell walls of diatoms consist of two box-like parts or valves and contain silica. (Silica is found in sand and is the material that is melted to make glass.) Diatomaceous earth is an earthy deposit formed from the shell-like skeleton of diatoms and is made into a finely powdered form as an absorbent or filter material. It is used in swimming pool filters and in gardening.

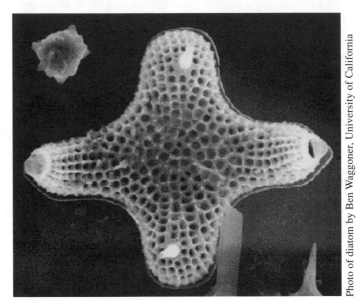

Photo of diatom by Ben Waggoner, University of California at Berkeley

Erosion and the Science of Geology

Descriptions of erosion and the way rivers carry sand and clay to the sea can be found in the writings of a number of ancient Greek and Roman philosophers, including Herodotus and Aristotle. The records of a large number of ancient civilizations note the problem of erosion and its adverse effects on agriculture. But it was not until the mid-1700s that our current geological theories began to be developed.

One of the foremost contributors to modern-day geology was a Scottish physician named James Hutton, who published a book entitled *Theory of the Earth with Proof and Illustrations*. Hutton argued that "the present is the key to the past," and he used his observations of the Scottish countryside to oppose theories current at that time which considered changes in the Earth's surface to be mainly the result of catastrophes like floods and earthquakes. Hutton argued that the Earth's surface is much more affected by gradual, uniform processes taking place over long periods of time. One of his chief interests was the effect of moving water on the Earth's surface. He described each stage of the erosion cycle. Hutton's writings had a profound influence on later geologists, such as the British scientist Charles Lyell in the mid-1800s who used scientific measurements of the amount of sediment in rivers to show that erosion is a constant process. Today it is accepted that both slow, uniform processes and catastrophic events are important in shaping the Earth's surface.

By the turn of the century, these investigations were greatly enhanced by the work of a Harvard University geologist named William M. Davis. Davis was the first to point out that rivers are like living organisms that grow from infancy through youth and maturity to old age. He described the differing features of a river during all of these stages and his theories are still very much in use today. He described the cycle of erosion from waterfalls and rapids with V-shaped, separated valleys, to wider valleys and many tributaries, to a much flatter landscape with a wide meandering river. Several of the books in the "Resources" section contain diagrams or drawings of the erosion cycle as described by Davis.

One very interesting spin-off from Davis' work was proposed by an American engineer named Robert E. Horton. He applied mathematics and statistics to the classification of rivers, especially in regard to the complexity of their tributary system. He designated a stream with no tributaries as of the "first order" of magnitude; a river with one or more first-order tributaries was of the "second order." A "third order" river has to have at least one "second order" tributary. Under Horton's system, the Mississippi is about 10th order, while the Amazon and the Congo are classified as 12th or 13th order. If any of your students are so inclined, they may want to pursue an independent project about Horton's work because it led to a recognition of a surprisingly consistent mathematical relationship in all rivers between the river and its number of tributaries.

All of this early geological pioneering about river systems led to the application of physics to the energy of rivers and the entire water cycle, to the thermodynamics of rivers, and even to increased understanding of why all rivers have a tendency to meander.

In addition to learning more about rivers and river features, your students may want to pursue a number of related and fascinating fields of interest. These include early theories about the movement of ice that led to a better understanding of Ice Ages and the Earth's climate, the role that wind plays in the earth-carving process, and the incredible caverns sculpted beneath the Earth by underground water flow.

Resources

There are a great many books, videos, and other instructional materials about rivers, the water cycle, and the earth sciences. Following is a selection of the items we've found most useful. A search of your school or city library will undoubtedly turn up many others.

Books

Book of Planet Earth, Martyn Bromwell, Simon and Schuster, New York, 1992. A little larger than a field guide, this book uses photographs and diagrams to depict the forces shaping Earth's landscapes.

Cadillac Desert: The American West and Its Disappearing Water, Marc Reisner, Penguin Books, New York, 1987. This is a thorough and fascinating story of state and federal water projects in the western United States.

Chiseling the Earth: How Erosion Shapes the Land, by R.V. Fodor, Enslow Publishers, Inc., Hillside, New Jersey, 1983.

Dorling Kindersley Science Encyclopedia: The Earth, An Introduction to Physical Geology, Edward J. Tarbuck and Frederick K. Lutgens, MacMillan Publishing Co., New York, 1993. This has an excellent chapter on geological forces shaping landscapes.

Geography of the Earth, Susan Brooks, Oxford University Press, London and New York, 1991. This children's atlas has nice illustrations of continents and landforms that show rivers and mountains.

Grand Canyon: The Story Behind the Scenery, by L. Greer Price, KC Publications, Las Vegas, 1991. Through large color photographs, river diagrams, and information about geological formations, this book describes the Grand Canyon. The publisher carries a variety of books on natural sites nationwide Contact: P.O. Box 94558, Las Vegas, Nevada 89193-4558 (1-800-626-9673).

Heath Earth Science, Rolland B. Bartholomew and Bill W. Tillery, D.C. Heath and Company, Lexington, Massachusetts, 1984.

Historical Atlas of the Earth, Stephen Jay Gould, Roger Osborne, and Donald Tarling, Henry Holt Reference Book, Henry Holt & Co., 1996. This large beautifully illustrated book describes the evolution of Earth landscapes from the beginning of the solar system to the present. Constructive and destructive forces shaping the surface are shown, as well as the evolution of life and ecosystems.

The Pebble in My Pocket, A History of Our Earth, Meridith Hooper and Chris Coady, Viking Penguin Books, New York, 1996. This children's book depicts the travels of a pebble from a volcano 480 million years ago to the present.

Water, Luna B. Leopold, Kenneth S. Davis, and the Editors of *LIFE*, Life Science Library, Time Incorporated, New York, 1966.

Weather, David Ellyard, Nature Company Discoveries Library, Time Life Books, New York, 1995. This book has beautiful photographs and diagrams of the influence of weather on land surfaces.

Articles

"Do We Treat Our Soil Like Dirt?" by Boyd Gibbons, *National Geographic*, Volume 166, Number 3, September, 1984, pages 351–388. This is an outstanding article on erosion and the human impact on soil, with numerous related features, illustrations, and photographs. A color map of the United States shows the soil groups that predominate by region. Striking illustrations and close-up photographs show the denizens of the soil and explain their interconnections with it.

Internet

The photographs of landforms in this guide were obtained from a collection of images on the World Wide Web, designed for use by teachers. These images can be accessed at: http://www.GeoImages.berkeley.edu/GeoImages.html

The U.S. Geological Survey offers a variety of services via the Internet, including maps and images. These services can be accessed at the USGS GeoData home page at: http://www.usgs.gov/

Information about diatoms can be obtained from the following locations:
• Diatom Home Page
http://www.indiana.edu/~diatom/diatom.html
• Introduction to the Bacillariophyta
http://www.ucmp.berkeley.edu/chromista/bacillariophyta.html
• Bowling Green State University Diatom Image Archive
gopher://gopher.bgsu.edu/1/Departments/biol/algae

Other Instructional Materials

Aerial photographs of your region, which reveal rivers and water drainage patterns, can be obtained from the National Aerial Photography Program (NAPP). You can order directly by sending a map outlining your area of interest to one of the two addresses below, or calling 1-800-USA-MAPS.

Sioux Falls—ESIC   OR   USDA—ASCS
U.S. Geological Survey   Aerial Photography Field Office
Sioux Falls, SD 57198   P.O. Box 30010
2222 West 2300 South
Salt Lake City, UT 84130-0010

"America By Air." This video series, originally broadcast on PBS, is available at some libraries with video collections. Wonderful aerial footage of rivers and geological features is provided in each of the productions, making a great connection for your students to the ways their river models compare to the bird's eye view of the natural world.

Water Matters Guide and Poster by Sue Cox Kauffman, NSTA Special Publications, printed by Automated Graphic Systems, Stock Number: PB116X1, ISBN: 0-87-355-127-3, 1994. *Water Matters* includes a water resources teacher's guide in several volumes that provides background information on a wide variety of topics, such as biodiversity, watersheds, acid rain and hazardous materials, wetlands, and water use The guide includes lessons designed to consider the national science standards. The sets of posters include wonderfully illustrated maps for students to visualize from a bird's eye view. The poster information on ground water contamination is ideal for the toxic waste activity in *River Cutters*. *Water Matters* is available from:

National Science Teacher's Association
1742 Connecticut Avenue NW
Washington, D.C. 20009   OR
(202) 328-5800

American Water Resources Association
5410 Grosvenor Lane, Suite 220
Bethesda, Maryland 20814-2192
(301) 493-8600

Watershed-Related Resources

There are many river and stream projects across the country that focus on environmental issues and education about regional watersheds. The Adopt-A-Stream Foundation has a handbook, *Adopting A Stream*, published by the University of Washington Press. The Oregon Department of Fish and Wildlife has a resource called *The Stream Scene: Watersheds, Wildlife, and People* with some excellent activities in the section entitled, "Does the Earth Wear a Raincoat?" There is a national Adopt-A-Watershed program, based in Hayfork, California, that distributes packets of educational materials to schools nationwide—so students from early grades through high school can learn about and track their local watershed throughout their school careers. Several GEMS guides are distributed by Adopt-A-Watershed. For more information, call (916) 628-4212. The International Rivers Foundation and poet Robert Hass sponsor an annual "River of Words" poetry and poster contest that your students may be interested in entering. Contact the International Rivers Network at (510) 433-7020. See the poem by Robert Hass on page 54.

Interactive CD-ROM

Exploring the Nardoo: An Imaginary Inland River Environment to Investigate, Maintain and Improve, published by Interactive Multimedia Pty Ltd., 1996. Designed for Grades 6–10, this multimedia CD for Macintosh or Windows simulates a changing inland river catchment, from pristine past to present development-affected state. Students explore the ecology of this imaginary environment through four physical regions—from high in the mountains to the plains below—and see how these regions change across four time periods. Students can conduct tests and visit the "Water Research Centre" to find information from many sources, then conduct an investigation they choose from the "River Investigations" noticeboard. For more information, contact: The Learning Team, 84 Business Park Drive, Armonk, New York 10504, (914) 237-2226 or call (800) 793-TEAM.

Nile: Passage to Egypt, from Discovery Communications, 7700 Wisconsin Avenue, Bethesda, Maryland 20814-3522, (301) 986-1999. Sanua is your guide on a journey 4000 miles long and 5000 years back in history. Lots of information, as well as games, mathematics, and technology connections.

Assessment Suggestions

Selected Student Outcomes

1. Students improve in their abilities to accurately identify geological features, and to explain how flowing water creates these features over long periods of time.

2. Students demonstrate an increased understanding of rivers as dynamic, changing systems that evolve over time.

3. Students gain further knowledge of erosion, weathering, and deposition, as some of the most important processes that shape the surface of the Earth.

4. Students demonstrate their abilities to use models to simulate a flowing river, including the ability to accurately observe and record changes in their models over time, and to recognize both the values and limitations of models to learn about natural systems.

5. Students improve in their abilities to design, conduct, and evaluate controlled experiments.

6. Students gain an increased understanding of how human intervention impacts the environment and how scientific models and investigations can contribute further knowledge and suggest possible solutions to unforeseen consequences.

Embedded Assessments

A variety of suggestions are provided in this Teacher's Guide to enable you to assess student progress toward the outcomes listed above. These include questions that will help you find out your students' ideas before instruction, as well as both questions and activities that will enable you to assess their level of understanding during and after instruction. These assessment suggestions are embedded in the text, so that they become an integral part of instruction.

We do not give specific remedies to employ if your students do not grasp the concepts as deeply as expected. It will be up to you, as a sensitive and insightful teacher, to determine the ideas that your students have not yet grasped, and to decide if it best to revisit these in a discussion, or to emphasize them in the lessons to follow. In general, if your students do not understand a key idea, it is best to revisit that idea through additional discussions or activities such as those listed in the "Going Further" sections, before going on to an entirely new topic. Following is a list of the assessment suggestions provided in the *River Cutters* teacher's guide.

Pre-Instruction Questions. There are several opportunities in this teacher's guide to find out your students' ideas **prior to instruction.** In each case, the ideas that your students offer can help you to "fine-tune" the instruction to address their particular needs. For example:

Questions about how water shapes the land are asked before instruction begins in Session 1. Students are asked to discuss their ideas about how local landforms were created, the role that water has played in shaping the land, and how long they think it took for the local terrain to take its present form. Throughout the session, there are other opportunities to find out the students' preliminary ideas as they set up and use their river cutter tubs.

Questions about erosion, weathering, and deposition. A series of questions are suggested in Session 2 that will enable you to find out your students' ideas first, just before introducing the concepts of erosion, weathering, and deposition. This "Socratic" approach—introducing new ideas through questions—enables you to adjust the presentation to your students' growing understanding. (Outcome 3)

Questions about the use of models. At the end of Session 2, a series of questions reveals what your students understand about the strengths and limitations of models in reflecting natural processes. (Outcome 4)

Questions about controlling variables. At the end of Session 5, before they are introduced to controlled experimentation, the students are asked why they think the time for each river run was kept the same for all teams. In Session 6 they are asked for their ideas about how they might test alternative theories about the formation of river valleys before being introduced to controlled experimentation. (Outcome 5)

Post-Instruction Questions. There are also opportunities to find out how much your students learned as a result of instruction. For example:

Questions about how water shapes the land. Session 2 begins with a series of questions in which students imagine they are tiny travelers, walking along the rivers in their models. Through these questions you can determine whether or not your students are connecting the features they observed in their models with real geological features. Additional questions about the formation of geological features over time are asked in Sessions 3, 4, and 5. At the end of Session 6, students are asked to apply the results of the experiments so far to local landforms. (Outcomes 1 and 2)

Questions about human intervention. In Session 4, students are asked to interpret the results of their activities with dams and toxic waste dumps. These questions illustrate what they have learned from the models, and also what they already know about the effects of these human interventions on river systems. Students answer further questions to compare natural processes with human interventions at the beginning of Session 5. (Outcome 6)

Questions about the use of models. At the conclusion of Session 6, students are asked what would happen if they changed their models by running them longer, and about the use of models for conducting controlled experiments. (Outcome 4)

Questions about controlling variables. In Session 6, students are asked to distinguish between systematic observations of models and controlled experiments. They are also asked to identify test variables. At the conclusion of Session 7, students are asked to interpret the results of their own controlled experiments or investigations. They are also asked how they would improve the experiments. (Outcome 5)

Activities. In addition, what students do during class activities provides a rich source of information on their level of understanding. For example:

River Features Flags. Students use small flags to label river features on their model rivers as they begin Session 4. Their labeling and placement of the flags in Session 4 and subsequent sessions provides information about their understanding of terminology and knowledge of geologic features and how features change over time. (Outcomes 1, 2, and 3)

River Models and Student Drawings. Throughout the unit, the students' river models and drawings provide information about their growing knowledge of river features, and their abilities to use the model to study natural systems. (Outcomes 1, 2, 3, 4, 5, and 6)

Design Your Own Experiments. The culminating activity is found in Session 7, in which students design their own experiments. This is a "full investigation" as described in the *National Science Education Standards* (1996). The plans handed in by each group, and the lab report completed by teams or individuals, will provide evidence of the students' understanding of systematic observation and controlled experimentation, their use of models to answer their own questions, and their abilities to draw valid conclusions from the results of their experiments. Various projects are also likely to reveal students' understanding of the subject matter, including: geological features, how rivers change over time, and the effects of human intervention. (Outcomes 4, 5, and others, depending on the experiments selected.)

Additional Assessment Ideas

How was our local landscape formed? The students describe their own theories about how the local landscape was shaped by water. They also describe how they might use a model to test their theories. Compare the students' ideas at the end of the unit with the ideas they expressed in the first session. How much have their ideas changed? (Outcomes 1–4)

Describe A Real River Visit. Have students write a paragraph about a river area they have visited, describing various geologic features that they observed. After they have finished their descriptions, students can compare their own river model with the real river area. (Outcomes 1, 2, 3, 4)

Create-A-River-Legend. Have students write an imaginary legend or story that explains why the Earth's surface is shaped as it is. The story can have whatever characters and events the students decide, but it must include a character who represents the power of water. The story might also describe how the river has been affected by humans. (Outcomes 1, 2, 3, 4, 6)

Design A Travel Brochure. Have your students design a promotional brochure to advertise the natural beauty, geologic features, and tourist attractions of their own river area. You can review these brochures for use of terminology, descriptive detail, understanding of river systems, and human impact. (For a detailed case study of the travel brochure assessment with actual student work shown and evaluated, see *Insights and Outcomes: Assessments for Great Explorations in Math and Science*, the GEMS assessment handbook.) (Outcomes 1, 2, 3, 4)

Letter to the Editor. Have students write a letter to the editor of a local newspaper that takes a strong position on a controversial river-related issue. The letter should state clearly what the writer thinks should be done and why. (Outcomes 1, 6)

Here's an example of such an issue:

> You live on the shore of a large river. Two previously unknown toxic waste dumps have been unearthed 25 miles upstream from your home, both about 200 yards away from the river's shoreline. Meanwhile, a small dam project to bring water to several new housing developments is being planned about 20 miles upstream. You are very concerned that there has not been enough discussion about the toxic waste dumps and, furthermore, that no one even seems to question whether or not the dam construction might make matters worse. You recommend in your letter that work on the project be stopped until a thorough study of the site is completed and a model is built to test the effect of the planned changes.

Literature Connections

The Adventures of Huckleberry Finn
by Mark Twain
Viking Penguin, New York. 1953
Grades: 6–Adult

> A boy and a runaway slave start down the Mississippi on a raft in this exciting and sometimes dangerous trip. The Mississippi courses through much of Twain's work, even in his pen-name itself (from a riverboat working command). While the language and dialect reflect their time and can be discussed in class, Twain's essential humanity comes through.

Biography of a River: The Living Mississippi
by Edith McCall
Walker and Co., New York. 1990
Grades: 6–12

> This "biography" details the history of human interactions with the Mississippi, from Native Americans, European expeditions, and U.S. acquisition through recent engineering projects. The river "speaks" in the first person in the opening chapter. Discussion of engineering relates to dam building challenges in *River Cutters*. The emphasis on the "living" nature of the river underlines an important environmental lesson.

Danny Dunn and the Universal Glue
by Jay Williams and Raymond Abrashkin; illustrated by Paul Sagsoorian
McGraw-Hill, New York. 1977
Grades: 4–9

> Danny and friends bring evidence to a town meeting which indicates that waste from a local factory is polluting the local stream. A discussion of watersheds, water tables, and the way pollution moves through the system of streams relates well to the toxic waste activity.

Drylongso
by Virginia Hamilton; illustrated by Jerry Pinkney
Harcourt, Brace, Jovanovich, San Diego. 1992
Grades: 2–6

> This book takes a powerful look at what happens when rivers dry up. An unknown boy blows into a village with a severe dust storm, and tells the villagers his name is Drylongso. He has special information about drought cycles, agriculture, and ways to survive; he carries a "dowser," or divining rod. This book contains excellent information on climate, drought, drought cycles, and soil conditions.

Love Canal: My Story
by Lois M. Gibbs
State University of New York at Albany Press,
Albany, New York.   1982
Grades: 6–12

> Autobiography of the housewife who organized a
> neighborhood association that eventually resulted in a clean up
> of the Love Canal toxic waste site and relocation of the families
> living there. She went on to form the Citizen's Clearinghouse
> for Hazardous Waste based in Arlington, Virginia.

Minn of the Mississippi
by Holling Clancy Holling
Houghton Mifflin, Boston. 1951
Grades: 6–12

> The journey of Minn, a snapping turtle, is followed from
> northern Minnesota to the bayous of Louisiana. Her adventures
> with people, animals, and the changing seasons are vividly
> described. Wonderful drawings and maps of her travels
> accompany the engaging true-life story on the Mississippi River.
> Newbery honor book.

The Missing 'Gator of Gumbo Limbo: An Ecological Mystery
by Jean C. George
HarperCollins, New York. 1992
Grades: 4–7

> Sixth-grader Liza K and her mother live in a tent in the Florida
> Everglades. She becomes a nature detective, searching for
> Dajun, a giant alligator who plays a part in a waterhole's
> oxygen-algae cycle, and is marked for extinction by officials.
> The book details local habitats and species. "Look how Mother
> Nature's plan for the Everglades has been tortured and
> diverted...the Everglades, which is really a slow river, is so rich
> with soil and nutrients that the Army Corps of Engineers was
> engaged to drain it for farmland..." Her neighbor explains how
> canals were built, fish and birds died, and the river changed.
> "You change one thing and you change the whole ecosystem."

Our Endangered Planet: Rivers and Lakes
by Mary Hoff and Mary M. Rogers
Lerner Publications, Minneapolis. 1991
Grades: 4–9

> An attractive and user-friendly reference book covering the
> dangers of surface water pollution with many illustrations and
> photographs. Other relevant titles in this series (all published
> in 1991) include: *Groundwater, Population Growth*, and *Tropical
> Rain Forests*.

Paddle-to-the-Sea
by Holling Clancy Holling
Houghton Mifflin, Boston. 1941
Grades: 6–9

> A Native American boy carves a wooden figure in a canoe and sets it afloat near the headwaters of a river north of the Great Lakes. This book chronicles the canoe's four-year journey to the sea. Caldecott honor book. (A detailed review of this book follows this section, on page 89.)

Rain of Troubles: The Science and Politics of Acid Rain
by Lawrence Pringle
Macmillan, New York. 1988
Grades: 5–12

> Acid rain's discovery, formation, transportation, its effects on plant and animal life, and how economic and political forces have delayed action are discussed. The impact of acid rain on lakes and rivers can be related to the toxic waste modeling activities in this guide

A River Ran Wild: An Environmental History
by Lynne Cherry
Harcourt, Brace, Jovanovich, San Diego. 1992
Grades: 1–5

> True story of the Nashua River Valley in North-Central Massachusetts from the time that the Native Americans settled there, naming it River With the Pebbled Bottom. The book traces the impact of the industrial revolution on the river and the eventual clean-up campaign mounted by a local watershed association. The graphic borders are packed with historical information, showing the original wildlife, tools and utensils used by Native Americans and early settlers, and continuing on to modern artifacts.

The River That Gave Gifts: An Afro-American Story
by Margo Humphrey
Children's Book Press, San Francisco. 1987
Grades: K–5

> Four children in an African village make gifts for wise old Neema while she still has partial vision. Yanava, who is not good at making things, does not know what to give, and seeks inspiration from the river. As she washes her hands in the river, rays of light fly off her fingers, changing into colors and forming a rainbow. After all the other gifts are presented, she rubs her hands in the jar of river water she has brought and thus gives a rainbow of light and the gift of sight to Neema. In addition to the themes of respect for elders and the validity of different kinds of achievement, the river is portrayed as a primeval source of power.

Sierra

by Diane Siebert; illustrated by Wendell Minor

HarperCollins, New York. 1991

Grades: 4–8

> This is a long narrative poem in the voice of a mountain in the Sierra Nevada. It begins and ends with the lines: *I am the mountain/ Tall and grand/ And like a sentinel I stand.* Dynamic verse and glorious mural-like colored illustrations depict the forces shaping the earth as well as the plant, animal, and human roles in this ecosystem.

Three Days on a River in a Red Canoe

by Vera B. Williams

Greenwillow/William Morrow, New York. 1981

Grades: 3–6

> Mom, Aunt Rosie, and two children on a three-day camping trip by canoe, encounter currents, wild winds, a rainbow, a moose, and more.

The Wind in the Willows

by Kenneth Grahame; illustrated by Ernest Shepard

Aerie Books, New York. 1988

Grades: 4–Adult

> This wonderful, humorous classic, filled with the bustling lives of eccentric animal characters, takes place along a river. The scenic descriptions accurately reflect the habitats of each animal. While the book is often read out loud to younger children, the pace and comic timing of the conversations makes it highly entertaining for adults.

Paddling to the Sea

River Cutters is a unit that enables students to model the passage of geological time, so they can simulate the effects of thousands of years of erosion in minutes. Students learn to identify geological formations, compare the features of old and young rivers, and investigate the effects of toxic waste dumps and dams on rivers, as they develop an understanding of river systems.

Paddle-to-the-Sea by Holling Clancy Holling (Houghton Mifflin, 1941, 1969) is the story of a small canoe, carved by a Native American boy, that makes a journey from a snow bank near a river to the north of Lake Superior all the way to the Atlantic Ocean. The boy sets out to test a theory:

"I have learned in school that when this snow in our Nipigon country melts, the water flows to that river. The river flows into the Great Lakes, the biggest lakes in the world. They are set like bowls on a gentle slope. The water from our river flows into the top one, drops into the next, and on to the others. Then it makes a river again, a river that flows to the Big Salt Water."

This enchanting book proceeds to chronicle the four-year journey of the carved boat, through rushing brooks, rapids, rivers, bays, canals, marshes, lakes and over waterfalls; through locks, a beaver dam, a sawmill, under docks, on boats, in storms, past factories. Over 50 pages long, this book is unusual in that every other page has a full-page color drawing. Margins are filled with little diagrams containing details of the Great Lakes, the path of the carved canoe, a diagram of a canal lock, some of the history of trade waterways, how a sawmill works, a diagram of a lake freighter, and more.

The story is full of picturesque language and lush detail of the wildlife surrounding the waters:

"A muskrat swam past the drifting canoe and disappeared in the dead rushes...A buck deer waded in the shallows. He had only one antler and the weight of it made him walk with his head turned aside...The cubs caught crayfish and frogs in the mud, while the mother bear squatted on a rock beside a deep pool in the lagoon and smacked a black bass to the bank with her paw."

The reader is filled with vibrant images of these inland waterways and all the life that relies on them. Both the ingenuity and the audacity of humans is clear as the carved canoe witnesses the positive and negative effects that food gathering, transport, and industry have had on our waters.

Reading *Paddle-to-the-Sea* can lead you and your students to a satisfying and rewarding conclusion to the GEMS *River Cutters* unit. Holling Clancy Holling has written several other books on related topics, including *Minn of the Mississippi*, about a turtle's journey. There are, of course, many other excellent books, including classics like *Wind in the Willows* and *Huckleberry Finn*, as well as more recent and environmentally conscious works, such as *A River Ran Wild* by Lynne Cherry.

Short Glossary of River and Related Features

Alluvial Fan: A deposit of sediment with a fan-shaped outline. Usually caused by a mountain stream losing velocity at the bottom of a slope, spreading out, and drying, or sinking into the soil.

Alluvial Plain: A flat area that borders a river where sediment is deposited when the river floods. Alluvial plains generally make rich farmland.

Aquifer: Water-bearing rock formations.

Bed Load: Sand, pebbles, rocks, or boulders that are moved along the bed of a stream but are too heavy to be suspended in the water.

Delta: The deposit formed at the mouth of a stream or river as it enters another body of water, slows its flow rate, and drops its load of sediment. Many deltas are triangular in shape, and the name derives from the triangular Greek letter.

Dendritic: From the Greek *dendron*, or tree, the name applies to the branching drainage patterns of streams and rivers.

Drainage Basin: The area of land drained by a river system.

Drainage Pattern: The pattern or arrangement formed by streams and their tributaries as they flow. Among major factors influencing the directions and patterns of drainage are the slope of the land, the structure and type of rock, and the specific geologic history of the region (effects of glaciers, volcanic, or other geologic activity). A deepening initial stream on a gentle slope tends to form a dendritic pattern, but a steeper slope or many other factors cause departures (trellis, radial, parallel) from this norm.

Eddy: A current of water moving in the opposite direction from the flow of the main stream.

Erosion: The moving or washing away of soil by water. Wherever water flows over soil, erosion is taking place. More generally, erosion is the wearing away of earth by streams, underground water, glaciers, wind, or the ocean.

Floodplain: A flat area or plain that borders a river or stream and is covered by water during time of flood.

Gully: Small valley-like formation often caused when heavy rain falls on a hillside.

Lake: A body of either fresh or salt water, of considerable size, surrounded by land. One of the ways lakes are created is when a stream is blocked, for example by a landslide. Lake basins can also be created by volcanic activity, as well as earth fault and glacial action.

Landslide: Sudden fall of a mass of loose rock down the side of a mountain, cliff, or hill.

Levee: A deposit of sand or mud built up along, and sloping away from, either side of the floodplain of a river or stream. Levees can be natural or built by people.

Meander: A rounded, or S-shaped bend or loop usually seen in an "older" or "mature" river.

Mouth: Part of a river where it flows into another body of water.

Ox-Bow Lake: A crescent-shaped lake formed from the curve or meander of a river, after the ends of the lake that originally met the river have been blocked or silted up.

Plunge Pool: A pothole or large depression formed at the base of a waterfall.

Pothole: A circular hole in the bottom or bedrock of a river caused by the grinding action of swirling sand or gravel.

Rapids: A part of a river or stream where the current runs very quickly.

River: A natural, fairly large, stream of water flowing in a course or channel, or in a series of channels.

Riverbank: The slopes of land bordering a river.

Riverbed: The channel in which a river flows or once flowed.

Sandbar: A shallow area in a river formed by the deposition of sediments. Sandbars can be made of sand, gravel, silt, mud, or a combination of these materials.

Sediment: Any loose material, including sand, mud, or gravel, that is washed off by erosion and carried by a river or other eroding force.

Source: The beginning or origin of a stream or river.

Spring: A natural source of water, rising from underground.

Stream Capture (or Stream Piracy): Diversion of the upper part of one river or stream by the forward, or headward, growth of another.

Stream Terraces: When changes in a river change its floodplain to a lower level, remnants of the old floodplain may remain in a terraced pattern.

Tributary: A stream that contributes its flow to a larger stream or river.

Valley: An elongated depression between uplands, hills, or mountains, especially one following the course of a river or stream.

V-shaped Valley: A valley with a V-shaped profile, carved by a river.

U-shaped Valley: A valley with a U-shaped profile, carved by a glacier.

Waterfall: A steep fall of water from a height, as over a cliff or precipice.

Watershed: The entire area drained by a river and its tributaries.

Water Table: The upper level of underground water in a region. Below the water table the ground is saturated with water.

Summary Outlines

Session 1: Exploring a Model River

Getting Ready

Before the Day of the Activity
1. Obtain and organize equipment and materials in advance.
2. Have students bring in magazine pictures of earth landscapes.
3. Read through information on diatomaceous earth, choosing a river flow system, and all Getting Ready instructions.
4. Select which type of dripper system you will use and make appropriate number for your class.
5. Prepare the river-cutting tubs.
6. Try out the activity yourself.
7. Duplicate "River Geological Features" handout.

On the Day of the Activity
1. Gather dripper systems and other materials.
2. Prepare diluted food coloring.
3. Settle the earth in tubs.

Introducing River Cutting
1. Tell students they'll be creating a model river and observing events that take place in it.
2. They will be using diatomaceous earth.
3. Show students the river cutting system.

Demonstrating How to Make a River
1. Set up a demonstration system, with the tub level.
2. Demonstrate how to set up dripper system; let it drip a little.
3. Help students visualize tub as a landscape. Ask, "If you were even smaller than a tiny ant, what features might you see along the river banks?"
4. Stop sample river and show students how to re-slope.

Students Explore the Model River
1. Organize teams and arrange desks/tables.
2. Let students feel and examine earth.
3. Have volunteer help pour blue water.
4. Have half of each team prepare tubs; other half set drip rate.
5. Circulate to ensure all students interact with materials and equipment.
6. Have teams start a five-minute "practice river."
7. Have teams stop dripper systems. Pairs of teams can share their experiences and results.
8. Outline clean up procedures. Use sponge to remove excess water; keep rivers intact for next session.

Session 2: Discussing River Features

Getting Ready

Before the Day of the Activity
1. Remind students to bring in pictures of landscapes.
2. Acquaint yourself with geology resources.

On the Day of the Activity
1. Assemble materials for making flags.
2. Have river-cutting tubs from the previous session nearby.

Discussing River Features
1. Students check river models and generate list of river features observed in previous session. Imagine again they are tiny travellers.
2. Encourage students to describe formations or river features.
3. After students' initial listing, distribute "River Geological Features" handout and photographs. Students work in pairs with these to identify further features that might appear in model rivers.
4. Reconvene class and ask them to add any new features.
5. Ask students if they have spent time along a real river and seen any of these features. How is model the same, different?

Processes That Build Up & Tear Down Landforms
1. Ask students for ideas on how surface of the earth gets built up over time, and list responses. These are "constructive" forces.
2. Ask how natural land forms were created. Define erosion.
3. Describe weathering.
4. Invite students to describe erosion/weathering they've seen in nature and their models.
5. Ask if anyone noticed areas where the river deposited some of the material it was carrying. Explain sediment.

What Do Models Tell Us?
1. Ask students to reflect on earlier ideas about how landforms are created.
2. Ask students to reflect on advantages and disadvantages of models.

Making River Feature Flags
1. Demonstrate how to cut index card into triangles for label.
2. Have teams cut cards to make triangles and label with features.
3. Set the flags aside for use in the next session.

Session 3: Time and the River

Getting Ready
1. Label containers for 10 historical events.
2. Make copy for each team of Past Events sheet; cut out events and place in containers; make overhead.
3. Make chalkboard or butcher paper timeline.

Setting the Scene: The Ice Age
1. Have students set up river models and start dripper systems at 2 drops per second.
2. Gather students away from models and explain that geological time is so vast it's hard to comprehend.
3. In the river model, one minute will represent 1,000 years. Show transparency of Earth 12,000 years ago and explain Ice Age conditions, glaciers, and the land bridge.

Carving Glacial Valleys
1. Use an ice cube to demonstrate how a glacier carves a valley.
2. Have students make their own glacial valleys, then start a river running through it, for 30 seconds (500 years). Have students draw the results.
3. Point out that valleys cut by rivers tend to be V-shaped; by glaciers, U-shaped.

Introducing the 12,000 Year Timeline
1. Ask questions to assist student observations of change over time.
2. Explain that the next activity will model 12,000 years.
3. Distribute a Timeline data sheet and explain that as you call out an event one student from each group will get a slip of paper describing the event. They should write the event on the timeline and describe changes they observe in their rivers.
4. Encourage students to observe and record carefully and consider allowing students to circulate to observe other models during gaps of several minutes in timeline announcements.

Discussion
1. Ask students how their rivers changed over long and short periods of time.
2. Show class the photo of Niagara Falls and read the caption.
3. Extend student understanding by explaining that 12,000 years is just the most recent phase of Earth's history—geological time extends back many millions of years.

Session 4: Dams and Toxic Waste

Getting Ready
Before the Day of the Activity
1. Cut 12–18 strips of acetate/plastic film to simulate dams.
2. Soak swabs in food coloring; allow to dry overnight.
3. In addition to river cutting setup, have ready flags, paper for recording observations, dams, and simulated toxic waste.
The Day of the Activity
1. Replenish supply of blue water.
2. Set up river-cutting systems.
3. Plan discussion area away from river systems.

Setting the Scene for the First River
1. Tell students to imagine diatomaceous earth is a continent sloping to seashore millions of years ago. The dripping water is the melting of the last glacier.
2. They will cut a five-minute river (5000 years) and document features. Then, they'll restart rivers to investigate effects of dams and toxic waste dumps.
3. Have each team select a timekeeper and a water watcher. Others can make additional flags as needed.
4. Demonstrate how to record observations.
5. After five minutes, flow is stopped; students draw map of river system.
6. Remind students not to interfere with river-cutting process.

Cutting the River
1. Have students start running their rivers.
2. Encourage/assist students as needed in planting markers.
3. After five minutes, encourage students to draw maps of the river and add more features. They should leave river intact.

Setting the Scene for Human Interventions
1. Explain that students will be engineers and geologists as they construct a dam and see what happens when toxic waste dumps are placed near a river.
2. Show students acetate strips as dams and demonstrate how to cut a notch to simulate a spillway.
3. Display red swabs to simulate toxic waste dumps. Demonstrate how to insert and mark.
4. Explain that movement of toxic waste through soil can be monitored by drilling test plugs with a clear plastic straw.

Observing Effects of Dams and Dumps
1. Have teams plan, then build dam and place toxic dumps.
2. When the dam and dumps are in place, the team can start its river flowing again to see what happens.
3. Circulate, asking questions to focus student observations.
4. Ask students to plot movement of toxic waste on maps.
5. Have students stop dripper systems and clean up. They should keep river systems intact for next session.

Session 5: Discussing the Results of River Models

Getting Ready
Have river-cutting tubs from previous session lined up.

Discussing the Results
1. Have students check their river systems from previous session, then get out maps and river feature lists.
2. Provide overview of session: first focus on how the rivers evolved over time, then share experiences with dams and toxic waste dumps.
3. Students add to list of features. As you record on class list, ask if the feature appeared in early or later stages of the river.
4. Have students brainstorm why some features appear when they do.
5. Have each team report the results of their investigations of dams, discuss benefits/problems.
6. Discuss environmental impact of toxic waste dump sites.
7. Debates are one good way to pose these questions. Encourage discussion. Ask questions to focus attention on time scale and uses of models.
8. Ask students for ideas about experiments to find out more about erosion, the effects of technology, and other factors of interest.

Session 6: River Experiments: Age or Slope?

Getting Ready
1. Assemble materials.
2. Set up the river model as in the previous sessions. Have students re-slope tubs.

What Are Your Students' Ideas?
1. Distribute Two River Valleys handout. Have students discuss the differences in the shapes of the two river valleys and write a few sentences explaining what they think caused the differences.
2. Invite students to explain their theories. If not brought up, mention both possible differences in the slope of terrain and differences in age.

Conducting Controlled Experiments
1. Challenge: to conduct an experiment to determine which factor, slope or age, is more likely explanation for differences between the two valleys.
2. Students run two river models side-by-side, one with wood propped underneath tub. All other variables kept the same.
3. Run rivers for five minutes, place feature flags, record features, and notice differences. Consider effects of slope.

What is the Effect of Age?
1. Ask students for predictions about how their rivers will change if they are run another 10 minutes.
2. Have students run the rivers for ten minutes and compare features, using flags to remember where features were in younger rivers.
3. Discuss effects of slope and age.
4. Provide additional information on sediments in both rivers.

Session 7: Designing Your Own Experiments

Getting Ready
Plan so there are several days between the planning session and the experimenting session, to gather any needed materials.

Students Plan Their Own Experiments (Period 1)
1. Students work in groups to plan their own river model investigations.
2. Hand out "Sample Research Questions" sheet to help focus discussion.
3. Tell students to complete a one-page summary to describe the question they wish to investigate, their plan for using the river models to address the question, and a list of any special materials.
4. Encourage class to brainstorm topics.
5. Explain that a question may need to be rephrased so it can be investigated.
6. Collect the summary from each group at the end of the class session. Read them over to assist with materials needs and make suggestions for improvements.

Conducting the Experiments (Period 2)
1. Circulate as groups conduct their investigations.
2. After each group has finished, ask for a short lab report stating the research question, procedure, results, conclusion, and recommendations.

Reporting the Results (Period 3)
1. Each group reports its results to the class.
2. Briefly summarize conclusions and list findings.
3. Explain how scientists and engineers use models to test theories and obtain practical information.
4. Encourage further questions and investigations.

Shen's Model Helps Undo 'Improvements' to a River

The largest ecological restoration project ever attempted in the United States will be guided in part by a model of a river built by Hsieh Wen Shen, professor of mechanical engineering and an expert on river dynamics.

Shen demonstrated his 60- by 100-foot model recently for the South Florida Water Management District officials who are directing the Kissimmee River Restoration Project, a $150 -$200 million Florida program to return the channelized river to its natural state.

Shen's three-year study will help officials decide the fate of the river that carries water from Lake Kissimmee to Lake Okeechobee in South Florida.

The Army Corps of Engineers channelized the river in the '60s, after earlier hurricanes whetted sediment for flood control. By 1971, the formerly shallow, meandering 98-mile river was a 52-mile canal. But the ecological impact proved devastating. Some 40,000 acres of wetlands disappeared, driving away 90 percent of the water birds.

Shen points out that his calculations have to take into account water flow under all circumstances. A system that drains water too quickly after intense rains could pose a natural disaster. —Jesús Mena

Reprinted from *The Berkeleyan*, a newspaper for faculty and staff of the University of California at Berkeley.

QUESTIONS

1. What do you think the "restoration project" is intended to accomplish?

2. What kind of information do you think Dr. Shen's model provided?

3. Imagine that you are in charge of the South Florida Water Management District. What questions would you ask Dr. Shen about his model?

4. Would data from Dr. Shen's model by itself be enough for you to decide what to do? If not, what other types of data might you need?

Hsieh Wen Shen (photo by Susan Spann)

The North Fork Is His Lab

The January 1997 California floods caused massive devastation to homes, roads, and farms. They also provided new information to scientists such as Jeffrey Mount, chairman of the geology department at the University of Caliornia at Davis, whose specialty is rivers. The North Fork of the American River serves as his laboratory, and the floods re-routed the river in major and unexpected ways. Mount told Charles Petit, science reporter for the San Francisco Chronicle: "As a geological event, these floods were not abnormal. They are a regular thing. It is the way the Earth sculpts itself." He said that studying in detail how the flood changed the landscape helps scientists find clues in ancient sedimentary rocks that provide important information on climate and landforms going back thousands, even millions, of years. Of course, studying flood effects can also give important practical help to people who live in regions where such floods may occur. He called the January flood "a colossal sedimentation event," explaining that a flood is not just a lot of water going downhill—rivers are full of sand, silt, and rolling boulders. He continued, "That's something engineers don't understand sometimes. It isn't only water in a channel. It is the dirt in the water that dictates its behavior." The suspended sediment adds to the river's scouring and sculpting power, changes its density and the way it flows over obstacles, and affects the "bedload" motion of its bottom layers of sand, gravel, and rocks. Mount was particularly surprised by the dramatic changes in course due to the flood, with the main channel of the river sometimes shifting 30 yards or more. He said, "I would have thought that a river gets in equilibrium with the shape of the canyon walls, and after a flood would settle back into pretty much the course it had." For Dr. Mount, whose lab is the fork of a river, this unexpected result is a good reminder that scientists (and science students) often have unexpected and surprising results—and that such results can lead to new understandings.

****

Geological Features

The river in the photo above has formed a *valley with a V-shaped profile.* Many rivers in V-shaped valleys have rapids and waterfalls.

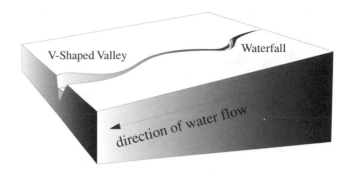

Above is a diagram of a *V-shaped valley.* The arrow shows which way the water is flowing.

The river in the photo at left flows through narrow *channels* in a shallow valley. The *floodplain* is the flat area that borders the river, which is covered with water in times of flooding. Sediment deposited on the floodplain probably comes from the mountains in the distance that show erosion *gullies* and *canyons.*

A rounded, or "S"-shaped bend or loop is called a *meander.* The river in the photo above flows in a meandering channel within a very wide, shallow valley. The valley floor is a large floodplain which is now rich farm land.

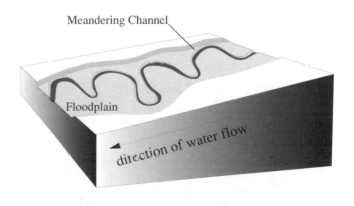

Above is a diagram of a wide, shallow valley. A *meandering channel* winds through the floodplain.

©1997 by the Regents of the University of California. LHS GEMS: *River Cutters.* May be duplicated for classroom or workshop use.

Geological Features (continued)

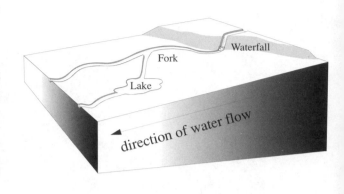

Waterfalls, like the one in the above photo, occur where the land through which a river flows drops rapidly. Some rivers, like the one shown in the diagram above and to the right, start out flowing rapidly in mountainous areas, then gradually slow when they reach shallower slopes, finally forming deltas when they reach the ocean. (The photo and diagram at the bottom of this page show deltas.)

An *alluvial fan* is a deposit of sediment that forms where a fast-flowing stream reaches more level land, spreads out, and is absorbed or evaporates. The small alluvial fans pictured to the left were deposited on sand dunes.

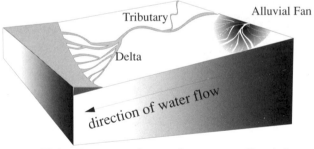

This diagram above shows an alluvial fan, a delta, and a *tributary,* which is a river that joins a larger river.

A *delta* is a deposit of sediment that occurs where a river or stream flows into a larger body of water. Deltas can be small, like the one pictured to the left, or large enough for entire cities to be built on them.

©1997 by the Regents of the University of California. LHS GEMS: *River Cutters.*
May be duplicated for classroom or workshop use.

The Earth Today

The Earth
During the Ice Age
12,500 Years Ago

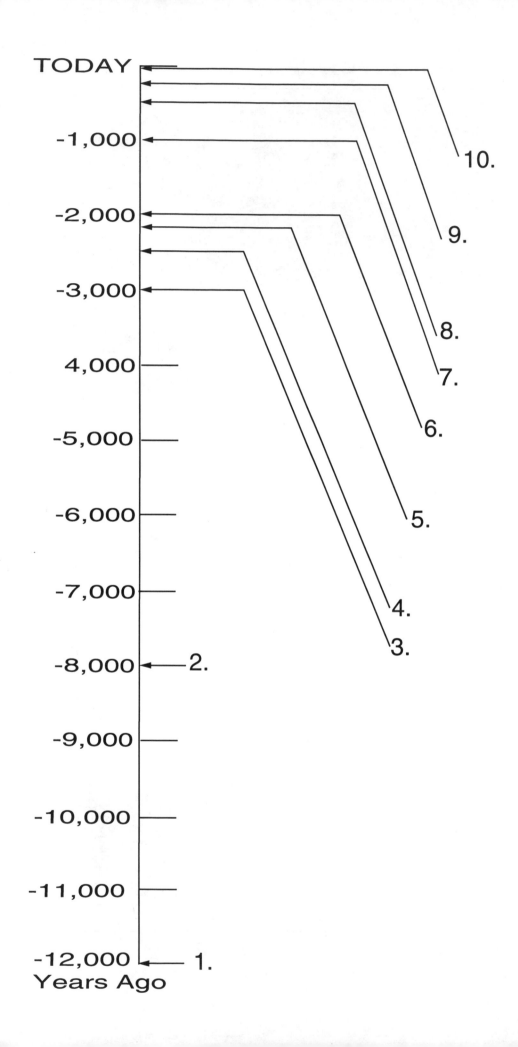

Timeline

TODAY

-1,000

-2,000

-3,000

4,000

-5,000

-6,000

-7,000

-8,000   2.

-9,000

-10,000

-11,000

-12,000   1.

Years Ago

10.

9.

8.

7.

6.

5.

4.

3.

Past Events

1. Land bridge migration takes place during ice ages, Last **Ice age ends** about 12,000 years ago. Mammoths and other large mammals begin to die off, possibly due to overhunting. **Increase drip rate to 5 drops/second.**

2. **Ice has melted** by about 8,000 years ago. After the end of the ice ages, the ice in North America has melted to present day levels. **Return drip rate to 2 drops/second.**

3. **Olmec** civilization flourishes in Mexico, approximately 3000 years ago. Unique stone monuments, statues, and designs have come down to us from Olmec culture.

4. **The Great Pyramid** was built in Egypt about 2,500 years ago, marking the zenith of a great ancient civilization.

5. **Great Wall of China**, about 2,200 years ago. The Emperor of the first united China ordered that a 4,000 mile long wall be built to protect against invaders.

6. **Roman Empire.** The Roman Empire was established in Europe, destined to have a powerful influence on the Western World.

7. **Ancient Ghana** was flourishing 1000 years ago in West Africa. Established hundreds of years before, this powerful kingdom was located to the north of the upper Niger River. (The modern nation of Ghana is farther south.)

Ancient Ghana

8. **Columbus sails** about 500 years ago, on his first voyage from Europe to the Americas. Native Americans have been there for thousands of years.

9. **United States established** about 225 years ago, with the signing of the Declaration of Independence.

10. **People land on the Moon** for the first time, about 30 years ago.

Past Events

1. Land bridge migration takes place during ice ages. Last **Ice age ends** about 12,000 years ago. Mammoths and other large mammals begin to die off, possibly due to overhunting. **Increase drip rate to 5 drops/second.**

2. **Ice has melted** by about 8,000 years ago. After the end of the ice ages, the ice in North America has melted to present day levels. **Return drip rate to 2 drops/second.**

3. **Olmec** civilization flourishes in Mexico, approximately 3000 years ago. Unique stone monuments and statues have come down to us from Olmec culture.

4. **The Great Pyramid** was built in Egypt about 2,500 years ago, marking the zenith of a great ancient civilization.

5. **Great Wall of China**, about 2,200 years ago. The Emperor of the first united China ordered that a 4,000 mile long wall be built to protect against invaders.

6. **Roman Empire.** The Roman Empire was established in Europe, destined to have a powerful influence on the Western World.

7. **Ancient Ghana** was flourishing 1,000 years ago in West Africa. Established hundreds of years before, this powerful African kingdom was located to the north of the upper Niger River. (The modern nation of Ghana is farther south.)

8. **Columbus sails** about 500 years ago, on his first voyage from Europe to the Americas. Native Americans have been there for thousands of years.

9. **United States declares its independence** about 225 years ago.

10. **People land on the Moon** for the first time, about 30 years ago.

©1997 by the Regents of the University of California. LHS GEMS: *River Cutters*

May be duplicated for classroom or workshop use.

Name_____

TWO RIVER VALLEYS

This is the Green River Valley in Colorado. It cuts deeply into the layers of rock and soil. The bank of the river is several hundred feet high.

photos by Lisa Weils, Vanderbilt University

This is the Sacramento River Valley in California. The banks of the river are just a few feet high. Frequent floods have made the surrounding farmland very fertile.

1. Compare these two meandering rivers. In your opinion, what might explain why one river has cut so deeply into the rock and soil, while the other river has cut a very shallow basin?

2. What evidence—from what you can see in the pictures, or from any experiments you may have done—supports your theory?

© 1997 by The Regents of the University of California. LHS GEMS: *River Cutters*.
May be duplicated for classroom or workshop use.

SAMPLE RESEARCH QUESTIONS

RESEARCH QUESTION: What happens if you build levees to control floods?

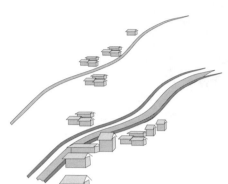

Having read about what happened during a large flood, a team of students decided to see if they could protect a city by building walls, or levees, on both sides of a river. They ran two rivers for five minutes, representing 5000 years. They then used extra diatomaceous earth to reinforce the banks of one of the rivers. They built a small city along the banks of both rivers, using houses from a Monopoly™ game. They then increased the rate of flow from the drippers and observed whether or not the towns were flooded, and how extensive the flooding was. They wanted to find out if the town with the levee "survived" with less flooding than the town without the levee.

RESEARCH QUESTION: How will plants affect erosion?

Some seeds will germinate and grow in diatomaceous earth. One group of students grew bean seeds in one part of a tub. (Grass and alfalfa seeds will also sprout in diatomaceous earth.) When the plants took root, they tilted the tub, and used a watering can equally on all of the surfaces. They watched to see if the area with the plants eroded more slowly than the area without the plants .

RESEARCH QUESTION: How do river meanders change over time?

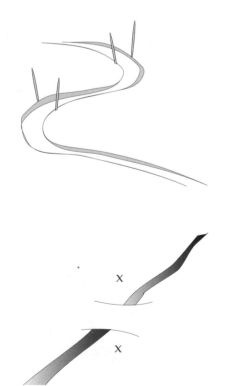

One group of students wondered whether meanders grew toward the outside or the inside of the curve. They also wanted to know if meanders traveled upstream or downstream over time. They decided to answer this question by observing and recording a river over a 20-minute period, to represent 20,000 years. One student was the timer. Another placed toothpicks on the inside and outside bends of meanders, while the others drew and took notes on what happened every two minutes.

RESEARCH QUESTION: What happens to toxic wastes in the soil?

Water below the surface of the ground is called the water table. In a dry riverbed, water may still be flowing underground where it can still be "tapped into" by plant roots and wells. One group of students decided to investigate this. They placed "toxic wastes" at several locations in their river model and let it run for a long time. They probed the entire tub to see what happened to it. They also dug wells and watched to see if these filled with toxic wastes.

© 1997 by The Regents of the University of California. LHS GEMS: *River Cutters*.
May be duplicated for classroom or workshop use.

Of Time and the River

by Lincoln Bergman

I.
How to imagine
The span of time
The erosion of earth
In stone called lime
The cutting of granite
Of soil or sand
Water, ice, wind
Their carving hand.

How to imagine
Time's vast flow
The dimmer it seems
The longer ago
And all that has happened
With humans on scene
Is scarcely a blip
On time's vast stream.

The raising of mountains
Earthquake, uplift
Glaciers scoop basins
Continents shift
Some changes are massive
Sudden and strong
Others take eons
Longer than long.

Vainly we seek
For the best metaphor
To open up time's
Immemorial door
To clearly explain
Such incredible scope
Billions of knots
On Earth's counting rope.

Imagine a flower
With petals unfurled
A beautiful rose
As big as the world
Each layer of petals
One million years old
Yet still there would be
Countless ages untold.

Imagine a valley
Winding and deep
Cut by a river
As we wake and sleep
Droplet by droplet
Inches to feet
Dried by the sun
Fed by the sleet.

Of time and the river
Great writers speak
Observing the ripples
Upon stream or creek
Caught, like us all,
In the great mystery
As time like a river
Flows to the sea.

II.
Time is a river
That flows to the sea
Carving the earth
Quite gradually

Time is a river
Flood on the rise
Changing the land
Before our eyes

Time is a river
An instant aware
Of leaping trout
Poised in air

Time is a river
Whose currents have seen
Dinosaur babies
Paddlewheel steam

Time is a river
It's all in the flow
Past, present, future,
Where does time go?

Time is a poem
Rhythm and rhyme
Time is a river
And rivers take time.

photo by G. Donald Bain, University of California at Berkeley